Ninja CREAMi

Cookbook

1500-Day Simple Cool Ninja CREAMi Recipes for Beginners and Advanced Users, With Ice Creams, Ice Cream Mix-Ins, Shakes, Sorbets, Smoothies, and More

Tricia Howard

Table of Contents

Introduction

Ice cream is one of the most famous and enjoyable treats worldwide. However, there are a lot of flavors of the ice cream, such as vanilla, strawberry, chocolate, peanut butter, cookies, and many more. It is hard to resist its sweet flavor, creamy texture, and refreshing coolness. Now, you can make ice cream at home. It is possible due to "NINJA CREAMI."

With "NINJA CREAMI," you can make not only ice cream but also you can make sorbet, gelato, smoothie bowls, milkshakes, lite ice cream, and your favorite flavored creams/topping like whipped cream etc. Spread creams over cakes, muffins, cupcakes, pies etc. It is super easy to use, and you don't need any special equipment to make ice creams. The cleaning process is super easy. The important accessories come with this kitchen appliance. You didn't need to purchase accessories for it. The size of "NINJA CREAMI" is perfect. You can put it on your kitchen counter. It will not take a lot of space.

Best of all, you can make diet ice creams. If you are on a vegan diet, then you can make ice cream with non-dairy milk such as soy milk, almond milk, or coconut milk as you want. In this cookbook, you will get different ice cream ideas and recipes. Select your favorite flavored ice cream and start making ice cream!.

What Is Ninja Creami?

NINJA CREAMI is a multi-functional kitchen appliance. You didn't need to purchase separate appliances for making smoothies, gelato, and ice cream. With NINJA CREAMI, you can make smoothie bowls, gelato, ice creams, sorbets, etc. It comes with different accessories such as creami pints, creami pint lid, motor base, creamerizer paddle, outer bowl, outer bowl lid, etc.

Benefits of Using Ninja Creami

Easy-To-Make Different Flavors:

Using NINJA CREAMI, you can make two, three, or six different flavors of ice cream. You cannot do it with a regular ice cream maker.

Super Simple Cleaning Process:

Containers, lids and paddle are dishwasher safe (top rack only). If you don't have a dishwasher, you can clean these accessories/parts with warm soapy water. Remember; don't use harsh chemicals to clean it.

Multiple Modes:

NINJA CREAMI is a multi-functional kitchen appliance. It has sorbet, ice cream, and gelato modes. You can make gelato (such as Italian ice cream), lite ice cream (such as diet ice creams), sorbet (such as processed or frozen fruit and vegetable juices), etc.

Make-Ahead Feature:

NINJA CREAMI has a make-ahead feature. It means you can use your favorite flavored base and place it in the freezer. Process the base in the NINJA CREAMI kitchen appliance when you want to eat it.

Quick Processing Time:

When ice cream gets frozen, NINJA CREAMI takes a few times to make the ice cream. The machine churns the ice cream mixture and transforms it into smoothie, sorbet, gelato, and ice creams.

Before First Use

Remove all packaging materials from the appliance. Rinse containers, lids, and paddle in warm and soapy water; clean the paddle with a dishwashing utensil. After thoroughly cleaning the accessories, you need air-dry them before use.
Wipe control panel with a soft cloth.

How Ninja Creami Works

Before using NINJA CREAMI, it is important to read how it is work. You should follow these steps if you want to make the ice creams.
Add ingredients in the CREAMI pint. Don't add ice or hard ingredients to it. Before making a smoothie, crush or thinly slice all fruits or vegetables.
Place ingredients in the pint and cover with a lid. Put it into the freezer. Then, place the pint container into the NINJA CREAMI.
Place the machine on clean, dry, and level surfaces such as the kitchen counter or table.
Remove the pint lid and set it in the outer bowl of the machine before refreezing it, level or smooth the surface of the base.
Insert the Creamerizer paddle in the bottom of the outer bowl. Release the lock.
Place the lid tab to the right of the outer bowl handle, aligning the lines on the lid and handle. Turn it clockwise to lock the lid.
Ensure the appliance is connected. Then, place the outer bowl onto the motor base. Turn the handle to the right to lift the platform and lock the bowl in position.
When the bowl is inserted, you will hear the sound "click." To turn on the appliance, press the power button. The NINJA CREAMI shows one-touch programs that create smoothies, sorbets, ice creams, gelato, and milkshakes with the touch of the button. Select the function.
When done, it will automatically turn off. The

machine will stop when the ice cream is done.

Unlock the lid and remove it. Add mix-ins in the hole of the pint. With the mix-ins program, add chopped mix-ins and repeat steps 6 to 10.

If you don't want to add mix-ins, re-spin can make a crumbly pint to make it creamier. RE-SPIN is often needed for very cold bases.

When done, remove the outer bowl and serve and enjoy!

Main Functions of The Ninja Creami

These functions are included in the NINJA CREAMI kitchen appliance:

ICE CREAM:

Ice cream mode is used for traditional indulgent recipes. This mode transforms dairy or non-dairy ingredients into thick, creamy, scoop-able ice creams. Such as vanilla, avocado, strawberry, blueberry, raspberry ice creams, etc. At home, you can create delicious ice creams for your family and friends. You can vegan ice cream using oat, almonds, or soy milk.

LITE ICE CREAM:

Lite ice cream mode is designed for health-conscious people. For example, if you want to eat low-sugar or sugar-substitute or low-fat ice creams, then lite ice cream is perfect. You can choose this program if you are on a keto, vegan, or paleo diet.

SORBET:

Sorbet mode is designed for making processed or frozen fruits and vegetables recipes with high water and sugar to transform into creamy and thick sorbets. For example, watermelon and mango ice cream, etc. This program makes perfect ice cream for vegans. Sorbets made in the CREAMI are incredibly smooth.

GELATO:

Gelato mode is designed for custard-based or Italian-style ice creams. This program is best when you have cakes, muffins, or cupcakes. Spread gelato over it. Gelato has a denser and smoother texture than regular ice cream.

SMOOTHIE BOWL:

This mode is designed for fresh or frozen fruits and vegetables with dairy, non-dairy, or dairy substitution products. For example, kale, blueberry, strawberry smoothie bowl, etc. A Smoothie bowl combines frozen fruits such as banana or blueberries, fresh fruits such as mango, strawberries, peaches, Minimal liquid or yogurt and protein powder if desired. You can top with your favorite topping such as granola, nuts, pistachios, shredded coconuts, etc.

MILKSHAKES:

This mode is designed to create quick and thick milkshakes. Combine ingredients, milk, and mix-ins in this process and select "MILKSHAKE" mode. For example, blueberry, apple, mango, raspberry milkshake, etc. If you want to drink thick milkshakes, this mode is perfect.

MIX-INS:

This mode is designed for giving the ice cream an extra flavor. Such as, you can add cookies, nuts, frozen fruits, cereals, chocolate and your favorite mix-ins. Remember, add chopped mix-ins in the NINJA CREAMI.

RE-SPIN:

It is designed for giving a smooth texture to the ice cream. It is used for very cold frozen fruits or vegetables. Re-spin is frequently needed when the base is cold (below −7 degrees F) and texture is crumbly instead of creamy.

Buttons and User Guide of Ninja Creami

You should know the operating buttons of NINJA CREAMI. Some of the essential buttons are following:

INSTALL LIGHT:

The Install light will glow when the appliance is not properly assembled. If the light is blinking, it means the bowl is properly installed. If it glows continuously, checks the paddle, it is properly installed.

PROGRESS BAR:

The progress bar shows the progress of the one-touch program. All four progress bar LEDs will flesh twice and then turn off when one program is complete.

ONE-TOUCH PROGRAM:

It is designed to whip up delicious creations in 1 to 2 ½ minutes. The programs vary in speed and length and it depends on the most favorable settings to get the best results according to the specific recipe.

Accessories and Components of Ninja Creami

These are the main accessories and components used to make the ice creams, sorbets, smoothies, and milkshakes.

CREAMI Pint:

Creami pints hold the ice cream base and then transform into smoothie, milkshake, gelato, sorbet, ice cream, and many more. You can store ice cream in these containers using CREAMI PINTS storage lids.

Motor Base:

It is a powerful motor base, and it is used to freeze the treats. Make sure that all parts are properly installed. It will process in 90 seconds.

Creamerizer Paddle:

The creamerizer paddle breaks the ice crystals for creamy and thick results. Make sure that creamerizer paddle is not bent or twisted.

Outer Bowl:

The outer bowl attaches the CREAMI pint to the motor base for processing.

Outer Bowl Lid:

The outer bowl lid fits on the outer bowl, and it holds the creamizer paddle.

CREAMI Pint Lid:

When ice cream is processed, use a creami pint storage lid to store it in the freezer.

Freezing Tips

Make sure that your freezer's temperature is adjusted properly. This unit is designed to process the base between 9 degrees F to -7 degrees F. If your temperature is within this range, your pint should reach the appropriate temperature.

You should freeze the base at least for 24 hours.

Place the pint on a surface level in the freezer, and don't freeze the pint at angle.

Uprights freezer are perfect. Chest freezer is not recommended as it will reach extremely cold temperatures.

Mix-In Tips

Add approximately ¼ cup of mix-ins – your favorite candies, cookies, frozen fruits, chocolate pieces, nuts, and more.

Hard mix-ins like chocolate, nuts, and candy are not processed during the mix-in program. Use mini chocolate pieces, small candies, chopped chocolate chips, etc.

After the MIX-INS program, soft mix-ins like cereals, frozen fruits, and cookies will be smaller. Use big pieces of frozen fruits and soft ingredients.

Don't use sauces, spreads, and fresh fruits for making gelato and ice creams because they will water down your treats. Nut butter is not mixed well. Use frozen fruits and caramel or chocolate shell toppings.

Don't use mix-ins while making milkshakes.

Cleaning and Maintenance of Ninja Creami

The cleaning process of NINJA CREAMI is pretty simple. Before cleaning, make sure to remove the Creamerizer paddle from the outer bowl.

Remove all parts from the appliance. Wash containers, paddles, and lids in warm soapy water.

Thoroughly rinse all parts. When all parts get dry, return to the main unit.

Containers, paddle and lids are dishwasher safe (top rack only).

Clean the main unit and paddle with a soft cloth.

Unplug the motor base before cleaning and clean it with a soft and moist cloth.

Don't use abrasive cloths or pads to clean the unit.

Strawberry Ice Cream

Preparation Time: 10 minutes|Servings: 4

Ingredients:

¼ cup sugar
1 tablespoon cream cheese, softened
1 teaspoon vanilla bean paste

1 cup milk
¾ cup heavy whipping cream
6 medium fresh strawberries, hulled and quartered

Preparation:
1. In a bowl, add the sugar, cream cheese, vanilla bean paste and with a wire whisk, mix until well combined. 2. Add in the milk and heavy whipping cream and beat until well combined. 3. Transfer the mixture into an empty Ninja CREAMi pint container. 4. Add the strawberry pieces and stir to combine. 5. Cover the container with storage lid and freeze for 24 hours. 6. After 24 hours, remove the lid from container and arrange into the Outer Bowl of Ninja CREAMi. 7. Install the Creamerizer Paddle onto the lid of Outer Bowl. 8. Then rotate the lid clockwise to lock. 9. Press Power button to turn on the unit. 10. Then press Ice Cream button. 11. When the program is completed, turn the Outer Bowl and release it from the machine. 12. Transfer the ice cream into serving bowls and serve immediately.

Serving Suggestions: Serve with the garnishing of chocolate wafers.
Variation Tip: Add vanilla chips to the mixture for added flavor.
Nutritional Information per Serving: Calories: 175|Fat: 10.5g|Sat Fat: 6.5g|Carbohydrates: 18.8g|Fiber: 0.4g|Sugar: 17.4g|Protein: 2.8g

Coconut Ice Cream

Preparation Time: 10 minutes|Servings: 4

Ingredients:

1 cup full-fat unsweetened coconut milk
2 tablespoons coconut, shredded

2 tablespoons whipped cream
⅓ cup granulated sugar

Preparation:
1. Add all the ingredients to a saucepan and simmer for 10 minutes over low heat. 2. Remove from the heat and let it cool. 3. After cooling, blend the mixture in a blender until smooth. 4. Transfer the mixture into an empty Ninja CREAMi Pint. 5. Cover the container with the lid and freeze for 24 hours. 6. After 24 hours, remove the lid and place the pint into the outer bowl of the Ninja CREAMi. 7. Install the Creamerizer Paddle onto the lid of the outer bowl, then rotate the lid clockwise to lock. 8. Turn the unit on. 9. Press the ICE CREAM button. 10. When the program is complete, turn the outer bowl and release it from the unit. 11. Serve in bowls.

Serving Suggestions: Top with caramel syrup.
Variation Tip: You can skip the cream.
Nutritional Information per Serving: Calories: 231|Fat: 17g|Sat Fat: 14g|Carbohydrates: 20g|Fiber: 1g|Sugar: 18g|Protein: 1.6g

Raspberry Extract Ice Cream

Preparation Time: 10 minutes|Servings: 4

Ingredients:

1 cup whole milk
¾ cup heavy whipped cream
½ teaspoon raspberry extract
¼ teaspoon lemon extract

½ teaspoon vanilla extract
4 drops blue food coloring
3 tablespoons granulated sugar

Preparation:
1. Beat all the ingredients in a bowl until combined. 2. Transfer the mixture to an empty Ninja CREAMi Pint. 3. Cover the container with the lid and freeze for 24 hours. 4. After 24 hours, remove the lid and place the pint into the outer bowl of the Ninja CREAMi. 5. Install the Creamerizer Paddle onto the lid of the outer bowl. 6. Rotate the lid clockwise to lock. Turn the unit on. 7. Press the ICE CREAM button. 8. When the program is complete, turn the outer bowl and release it from the unit. 9. Serve in bowls.

Serving Suggestions: Top with any fresh fruit.
Variation Tip: You can also use organic food coloring.
Nutritional Information per Serving: Calories: 72|Fat: 2g|Sat Fat: 1.2g|Carbohydrates: 11g |Fiber: 0g|Sugar: 12g|Protein: 2g

Pumpkin Gingersnap Ice Cream

Preparation Time: 15 Minutes|Cook Time: 24 Hours and 15 Minutes|Serves: 4

Ingredients:

1 cup heavy whipping cream
½ tablespoon vanilla extract
½ teaspoon ground cinnamon
½ teaspoon ground ginger
½ cup solid-pack pumpkin
1 (7 ounces) can Eagle Brand sweetened condensed milk
½ cup crushed gingersnap cookies

Preparation:

1. In a large mixing bowl, beat the heavy whipping cream, vanilla extract, cinnamon, and ginger with an electric mixer on medium speed until stiff peaks form. 2. Combine the pumpkin and sweetened condensed milk in a mixing bowl. 3. Add the crushed gingersnap cookies to the pumpkin mixture and stir well. 4. Pour the mixture into an empty ninja CREAMi Pint container and freeze for 24 hours. 5. After 24 hours, remove the Pint from the freezer. Remove the lid. 6. Place the Ninja CREAMi Pint into the outer bowl. Place the outer bowl with the Pint in it into the ninja CREAMi machine and turn until the outer bowl locks into place. Push the ICE CREAM button. 7. Once the ICE CREAM function has ended, turn the outer bowl and release it from the ninja CREAMi machine.

Serving Suggestion: Serve immediately.
Variation Tip: You can top the ice cream with crushed gingersnap cookies and chocolate syrup.
Nutritional Information per Serving: Calories 556|Protein 4.5g|Carbohydrate 36g|Dietary Fiber 1.4g|Sugar 25g|Fat 31g|Sodium 250mg

Pear Ice Cream

Preparation Time: 15 minutes|Cooking Time: 15 minutes|Servings: 4

Ingredients:

3 medium ripe pears, peeled, cored and cut into 1-inch pieces
1 (14-ounce) can full-fat
unsweetened coconut milk
½ cup granulated sugar

Preparation:

1. In a medium saucepan, add all ingredients and stir to combine. 2. Place the saucepan over medium heat and bring to a boil. 3. Reduce the heat to low and simmer for about ten minutes or until liquid is reduced by half. 4. Remove from the heat and set aside to cool. 5. After cooling, transfer the mixture into a high-speed blender and pulse until smooth. 6. Transfer the mixture into an empty Ninja CREAMi pint container. 7. Cover the container with storage lid and freeze for 24 hours. 8. After 24 hours, remove the lid from container and arrange into the Outer Bowl of Ninja CREAMi. 9. Install the Creamerizer Paddle onto the lid of Outer Bowl. 10. Then rotate the lid clockwise to lock. 11. Press Power button to turn on the unit. 12. Then press Ice Cream button. 13. When the program is completed, turn the Outer Bowl and release it from the machine. 14. Transfer the ice cream into serving bowls and serve immediately.

Serving Suggestions: Serve with the drizzling of caramel syrup.
Variation Tip: Make sure to use ripe pears.
Nutritional Information per Serving: Calories: 368|Fat: 18.5g|Sat Fat: 168g|Carbohydrates: 51.9g|Fiber: 4.9g|Sugar: 41.8g|Protein: 2.1g

Apple Pie Ice Cream

Preparation Time: 18 minutes|Servings: 4

Ingredients:

Non-stick cooking spray
2 cups apples, unpeeled and finely chopped (1–2 apples)
3 tablespoons water
3 tablespoons brown sugar
1 teaspoon vanilla extract
½ teaspoon ground cinnamon
½ cup heavy cream
½ cup apple cider

Preparation:

1. Spray a medium saucepan with non-stick cooking spray and place it over medium-high heat. Add the apples and water and cook for about 10 minutes, or until the apples are soft and the water has evaporated. 2. Add the brown sugar, vanilla, and cinnamon. Cook for an additional 2–3 minutes, or until the apples are very soft. 3. Transfer the cooked apple mixture to a large mixing bowl, then stir in the heavy cream and apple cider until everything is well combined. 4. Transfer the mixture to the Ninja CREAMi Pint. 5. Snap the lid on the pint and freeze it for 24 hours. 6. Remove the lid and assemble the unit as per the user instructions. 7. Select the ICE CREAM program. 8. When the program is complete, remove the outer bowl. 9. Serve in bowls.

Serving Suggestions: Top with apple slices.
Variation Tip: You can use any type of sugar.
Nutritional Information per Serving: Calories: 97|Fat: 5g|Sat Fat: 3g|Carbohydrates: 11g |Fiber: 0.2g|Sugar: 10g|Protein: 0.4g

Orange Ice Cream

Preparation Time: 10 minutes|Servings: 4

Ingredients:
½ cup milk
¾ cup heavy cream
⅓ cup orange juice
¾ cup sugar

Preparation:
1. Mix all the ingredients and beat until smooth. 2. Transfer the mixture into an empty Ninja CREAMi Pint. 3. Cover the pint with the lid and freeze for 24 hours. 4. After 24 hours, remove the lid and place the pint into the outer bowl of the Ninja CREAMi. 5. Install the Creamerizer Paddle onto the lid of the outer bowl, then rotate the lid clockwise to lock. 6. Turn the unit on. 7. Press the ICE CREAM button. 8. When the program is complete, turn the outer bowl and release it from the machine. 9. Serve in bowls.

Serving Suggestions: Top with orange zest.
Variation Tip: You can also use pineapple chunks.
Nutritional Information per Serving: Calories: 243|Fat: 9g|Sat Fat: 6g|Carbohydrates: 41g|Fiber: 0g|Sugar: 35g|Protein: 1.6g

Mocha Ice Cream

Preparation Time: 10 minutes|Servings: 4

Ingredients:
½ cup mocha cappuccino mix
1¾ cups coconut cream
3 tablespoons agave nectar

Preparation:
1. In a bowl, add all ingredients and beat until well combined. 2. Transfer the mixture into an empty Ninja CREAMi pint container. 3. Cover the container with storage lid and freeze for 24 hours. 4. After 24 hours, remove the lid from container and arrange into the Outer Bowl of Ninja CREAMi. 5. Install the Creamerizer Paddle onto the lid of Outer Bowl. 6. Then rotate the lid clockwise to lock. 7. Press Power button to turn on the unit. 8. Then press Ice Cream button. 9. When the program is completed, turn the Outer Bowl and release it from the machine. 10. Transfer the ice cream into serving bowls and serve immediately.

Serving Suggestions: Serve with the garnishing of almond slices.
Variation Tip: You can use fresh cream instead of coconut cream.
Nutritional Information per Serving: Calories: 297|Fat: 25.4g|Sat Fat: 22.3g|Carbohydrates: 19.2g|Fiber: 3.1g|Sugar: 15.4g|Protein: 2.5g

Cherry Ice Cream

Preparation Time: 10 minutes|Servings: 4

Ingredients:
1 cup cherries
⅔ cup heavy cream
½ cup sweetened condensed milk

Preparation:
1. Remove the stones from the cherries. In a food processor or blender, blend the pitted cherries until they are relatively smooth. 2. Whip the cream separately until medium-firm peaks form. 3. Mix the cherry puree and sweetened condensed milk into the cream until everything is well blended. 4. Transfer the mixture into an empty Ninja CREAMi Pint. 5. Cover the pint with the lid and freeze for 24 hours. 6. After 24 hours, remove the lid and place the pint into the outer bowl of the Ninja CREAMi. 7. Install the Creamerizer Paddle onto the lid of the outer bowl, then rotate the lid clockwise to lock. 8. Turn the unit on. 9. Press the ICE CREAM button. 10. When the program is complete, turn the outer bowl and release it from the machine. 11. Serve in bowls.

Serving Suggestions: Serve with cherries on top.
Variation Tip: You can also use milk and sugar instead of condensed milk.
Nutritional Information per Serving: Calories: 295|Fat: 18g|Sat Fat: 11g|Carbohydrates: 31g|Fiber: 1g|Sugar: 28g|Protein: 4g

Sesame Ice Cream

Preparation Time: 5 minutes|Servings: 4

Ingredients:
½ cup tahini
¾ cup unsweetened coconut cream
1 cup unsweetened soy milk
¼ cup raw agave nectar
Pinch of kosher salt

Preparation:
1. Combine all the ingredients in a blender and blend on high until smooth. 2. Transfer the mixture to the Ninja CREAMi Pint. 3. Snap the lid on the pint and freeze it for 24 hours. 4. Remove the lid and assemble the unit as per the user instructions. 5. Select the ICE CREAM program. 6. When the program is complete, remove the outer bowl. 7. Serve in bowls.

Serving Suggestions: Sprinkle sesame seeds on top.
Variation Tip: You can replace soy milk with whole milk.
Nutritional Information per Serving: Calories: 316|Fat: 21g|Sat Fat: 5g|Carbohydrates: 28g |Fiber: 3.2g|Sugar: 18g|Protein: 7.6g

Mango Ice Cream

Preparation Time: 10 minutes|Servings: 4

Ingredients:

¼ cup sugar
1 tablespoon cream cheese, softened
1 cup milk

¾ cup heavy whipping cream
2 mangoes, cut into very small cubes

Preparation:
1. Mix the sugar and cream cheese in a bowl. 2. Add the milk and heavy whipping cream. Combine well. 3. Transfer the mixture into an empty Ninja CREAMi Pint. 4. Add the mango cubes and stir to combine. 5. Cover the container with a lid and freeze for 24 hours. 6. After 24 hours, remove the lid. Place the pint in the outer bowl of the Ninja CREAMi. 7. Install the Creamerizer Paddle and lock the lid. Turn on the unit. 8. Press the ICE CREAM button. 9. When the program is complete, turn the outer bowl and release it from the machine. 10. Serve in bowls.

Serving Suggestions: Top with some more mango cubes.
Variation Tip: You can use frozen mangoes.
Nutritional Information per Serving: Calories: 265|Fat: 11g|Sat Fat: 6g|Carbohydrates: 41g |Fiber: 2.7g|Sugar: 38g|Protein: 4g

Burnt Sugar Ice Cream

Preparation Time: 15 minutes|Servings: 4

Ingredients:

3 eggs
1 cup unsweetened soy milk
½ cup unsweetened vegan creamer
¼ cup packed dark brown sugar

Pinch of kosher salt
¼ cup granulated sugar
1 tablespoon water

Preparation:
1. In a medium mixing bowl, whisk together the soy milk, creamer, brown sugar, salt, and eggs. 2. In a medium saucepan over medium heat, combine the granulated sugar and water and cook, stirring occasionally, until the mixture begins to caramelize, about 5 minutes. 3. When the sugar has caramelized, add the egg mixture in slowly, stirring gently to incorporate. 4. Remove the mixture from the heat and transfer it to the Ninja CREAMi Pint. 5. Snap the lid on the pint and freeze it for 24 hours. 6. Remove the lid and assemble the unit as per the user instructions. 7. Select the ICE CREAM program. 8. When the program is complete, remove the outer bowl. 9. Serve in bowls.

Serving Suggestions: Garnish with brown sugar on top.
Variation Tip: You can also use almond milk.
Nutritional Information per Serving: Calories: 192|Fat: 6g|Sat Fat: 2g|Carbohydrates: 27g |Fiber: 0.4g|Sugar: 26g|Protein: 8.2g

Lemon Ice Cream

Preparation Time: 10 minutes|Servings: 4

Ingredients:

1 (14-ounce) can full-fat unsweetened coconut milk
½ cup granulated sugar

1 teaspoon vanilla extract
1 teaspoon lemon extract

Preparation:
1. In a bowl, add the coconut milk and beat until smooth. 2. Add the remaining ingredients and beat until sugar is dissolved. 3. Transfer the mixture into an empty Ninja CREAMi pint container. 4. Cover the container with storage lid and freeze for 24 hours. 5. After 24 hours, remove the lid from container and arrange into the Outer Bowl of Ninja CREAMi. 6. Install the Creamerizer Paddle onto the lid of Outer Bowl. 7. Then rotate the lid clockwise to lock. 8. Press Power button to turn on the unit. 9. Then press Ice Cream button. 10. When the program is completed, turn the Outer Bowl and release it from the machine. 11. Transfer the ice cream into serving bowls and serve immediately.

Serving Suggestions: Serve with the garnishing of sweetened whipped cream and lemon zest.
Variation Tip: Granulated sugar can be replaced with sweetener of your choice.
Nutritional Information per Serving: Calories: 280|Fat: 18.3g|Sat Fat: 16.8g|Carbohydrates: 28.2g|Fiber: 0g|Sugar: 26.7g|Protein: 1.5g

Chocolate Ice Cream

Preparation Time: 10 minutes|Servings: 4

Ingredients:

1 cup almond milk
3 tablespoons cocoa powder
½ cup whipped cream
⅓ cup granulated sugar
1 teaspoon vanilla extract

Preparation:

1. Mix all the ingredients and blend until smooth. 2. Transfer the mixture into an empty Ninja CREAMi Pint. 3. Cover the container with the lid and freeze for 24 hours. 4. After 24 hours, remove the lid and place the pint into the outer bowl of the Ninja CREAMi. 5. Install the Creamerizer Paddle onto the lid of the outer bowl, then rotate the lid clockwise to lock. 6. Turn the unit on. 7. Press the ICE CREAM button. 8. When the program is complete, turn the outer bowl and release it from the machine. 9. Serve in bowls.

Serving Suggestions: Top with grated chocolate.
Variation Tip: You can use whole milk.
Nutritional Information per Serving: Calories: 256|Fat: 19g|Sat Fat: 15g|Carbohydrates: 22g|Fiber: 2g|Sugar: 18g|Protein: 2g

Earl Grey Tea Ice Cream

Preparation Time: 15 minutes|Cooking Time: 25 minutes|Servings: 4

Ingredients:

1 cup heavy cream
1 cup whole milk
5 tablespoons monk fruit
sweetener
3 Earl Grey tea bags

Preparation:

1. In a medium saucepan, add cream and milk and stir to combine. 2. Place saucepan over medium heat and cook until for bout two-three minutes or until steam is rising. 3. Stir in the monk fruit sweetener and reduce the heat to very low. 4. Add teabags and cover the saucepan for about 20 minutes. 5. Discard the tea bags and remove saucepan from heat. 6. Transfer the mixture into an Ninja CREAMi pint container and place into an ice bath to cool. 7. After cooling, cover the container with storage lid and freeze for 24 hours. 8. After 24 hours, remove the lid from container and arrange into the Outer Bowl of Ninja CREAMi. 9. Install the Creamerizer Paddle onto the lid of Outer Bowl. 10. Then rotate the lid clockwise to lock. 11. Press Power button to turn on the unit. 12. Then press Ice Cream button. 13. When the program is completed, turn the Outer Bowl and release it from the machine. 14. Transfer the ice cream into serving bowls and serve immediately.

Serving Suggestions: Serve with the garnishing of chocolate chips.

Variation Tip: You can use your favorite sweetener instead of monk fruit sweetener.
Nutritional Information per Serving: Calories: 140|Fat: 13.1g|Sat Fat: 8.1g|Carbohydrates: 3.6g|Fiber: 0g|Sugar: 3.2g|Protein: 2.6g

Blueberry Ice Cream

Preparation Time: 10 minutes|Servings: 4

Ingredients:

1 cup blueberries
½ cup vanilla whole milk Greek yogurt
¼ cup milk
2 tablespoons honey
2 tablespoons chia seeds

Preparation:

1. In a bowl, add all ingredients and eat until well combined. 2. Transfer the mixture into an empty Ninja CREAMi pint container. 3. Cover the container with storage lid and freeze for 24 hours. 4. After 24 hours, remove the lid from container and arrange into the Outer Bowl of Ninja CREAMi. 5. Install the Creamerizer Paddle onto the lid of Outer Bowl. 6. Then rotate the lid clockwise to lock. 7. Press Power button to turn on the unit. 8. Then press Ice Cream button. 9. When the program is completed, turn the Outer Bowl and release it from the machine. 10. Transfer the ice cream into serving bowls and serve immediately.

Serving Suggestions: Serve with the garnishing of fresh blueberries.
Variation Tip: Chia seeds can be replaced with flax seed.
Nutritional Information per Serving: Calories: 115|Fat: 4g|Sat Fat: 2g|Carbohydrates: 19.4g|Fiber: 2.2g|Sugar: 15.9g|Protein: 3.1g

Vanilla Ice Cream

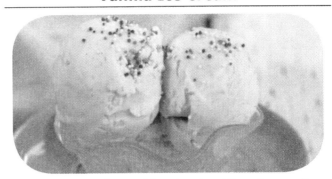

Preparation Time: 10 minutes|Servings: 6

Ingredients:

2 cups heavy whipping cream
2 cups half-and-half cream
1 cup sugar
2 teaspoons vanilla extract

Preparation:

1. Mix all the ingredients in a bowl. Stir until the sugar dissolves completely. 2. Transfer the mixture into an empty Ninja CREAMi Pint. 3. Cover the pint with the lid and freeze for 24 hours. 4. After 24 hours, remove the lid and place the pint into the outer bowl of the Ninja CREAMi. 5. Install the Creamerizer Paddle onto the lid of the outer bowl, then rotate the lid clockwise to lock. 6. Turn the unit on. 7. Press the ICE CREAM button. 8. When the program is complete, turn the outer bowl and release it from the machine. 9. Serve in bowls.

Serving Suggestions: Top with chocolate syrup.
Variation Tip: You can also use almond milk.
Nutritional Information per Serving: Calories: 308|Fat: 22g|Sat Fat: 14g|Carbohydrates: 23g|Fiber: 0g|Sugar: 23g|Protein: 3g

Carrot Cheesecake Ice Cream

Preparation Time: 10 minutes | Servings: 4

Ingredients:

1 cup heavy cream
½ cup carrot juice
⅓ cup light brown sugar
2 tablespoons cream cheese

frosting
1 teaspoon vanilla extract
1 teaspoon ground cinnamon

Preparation:

1. In a bowl, add all ingredients and beat until well combined. 2. Transfer the mixture into an empty Ninja CREAMi pint container. 3. Cover the container with storage lid and freeze for 24 hours. 4. After 24 hours, remove the lid from container and arrange into the Outer Bowl of Ninja CREAMi. 5. Install the Creamerizer Paddle onto the lid of Outer Bowl. 6. Then rotate the lid clockwise to lock. 7. Press Power button to turn on the unit. 8. Then press Ice Cream button. 9. When the program is completed, turn the Outer Bowl and release it from the machine. 10. Transfer the ice cream into serving bowls and serve immediately.

Serving Suggestions: Serve with the topping of chopped pecans.
Variation Tip: Use fresh carrot juice.
Nutritional Information per Serving: Calories: 185|Fat: 12.4g|Sat Fat: 7.3g|Carbohydrates: 18.4g|Fiber: 0.7g|Sugar: 15.8g|Protein: 0.8g

Mint Ice Cream

Preparation Time: 10 minutes | Servings: 8

Ingredients:

1 cup whole milk
¾ cup granulated sugar
2 cups heavy cream

2 teaspoons pure peppermint extract

Preparation:

1. In a bowl, whisk the sugar with the milk until it dissolves. 2. Stir in the heavy cream and peppermint. 3. Transfer the mixture into an empty Ninja CREAMi Pint. 4. Cover the pint with the lid and freeze for 24 hours. 5. After 24 hours, remove the lid and place the pint into the outer bowl of the Ninja CREAMi. 6. Install the Creamerizer Paddle onto the lid of the outer bowl, then rotate the lid clockwise to lock. 7. Turn the unit on. 8. Press the ICE CREAM button. 9. When the program is complete, turn the outer bowl and release it from the machine. 10. Serve in bowls.

Serving Suggestions: Top with chocolate shavings.
Variation Tip: You can also use coconut milk.
Nutritional Information per Serving: Calories: 211|Fat: 12g|Sat Fat: 12g|Carbohydrates: 24g|Fiber: 0.8g|Sugar: 23g|Protein: 2.3g

Coffee Ice Cream

Preparation Time: 10 minutes | Servings: 4

Ingredients:

¾ cup coconut cream
½ cup granulated sugar
1½ tablespoons instant coffee

powder
1 cup rice milk
1 teaspoon vanilla extract

Preparation:

1. In a bowl, add coconut cream and beat until smooth. 2. Add the remaining ingredients and beat sugar is dissolved. 3. Transfer the mixture into an empty Ninja CREAMi pint container. 4. Cover the container with storage lid and freeze for 24 hours. 5. After 24 hours, remove the lid from container and arrange into the Outer Bowl of Ninja CREAMi. 6. Install the Creamerizer Paddle onto the lid of Outer Bowl. 7. Then rotate the lid clockwise to lock. 8. Press Power button to turn on the unit. 9. Then press Ice Cream button. 10. When the program is completed, turn the Outer Bowl and release it from the machine. 11. Transfer the ice cream into serving bowls and serve immediately.

Serving Suggestions: Serve with the garnishing of sweetened whipped cream.
Variation Tip: You can use almond milk too.
Nutritional Information per Serving: Calories: 230|Fat: 11.2g|Sat Fat: 9.6g|Carbohydrates: 33.8g|Fiber: 1g|Sugar: 26.6g|Protein: 1.1g

Chia Seed Ice Cream

Preparation Time: 10 minutes | Servings: 4

Ingredients:

¼ cup milk
2 tablespoons honey
½ cup vanilla whole milk Greek

yogurt
2 tablespoons chia seeds

Preparation:

1. Mix all the ingredients and beat until smooth. 2. Transfer the mixture into an empty Ninja CREAMi Pint. 3. Cover the pint with the lid and freeze for 24 hours. 4. After 24 hours, remove the lid and place the pint into the outer bowl of the Ninja CREAMi. 5. Install the Creamerizer Paddle onto the lid of the outer bowl, then rotate the lid clockwise to lock. 6. Turn the unit on. 7. Press the ICE CREAM button. 8. When the program is complete, turn the outer bowl and release it from the unit. 9. Serve in bowls.

Serving Suggestions: Serve with any fruit.
Variation Tip: You can also use flax seeds instead of chia seeds.
Nutritional Information per Serving: Calories: 97|Fat: 2.7g|Sat Fat: 0.8g|Carbohydrates: 14.4g|Fiber: 2g|Sugar: 11g|Protein: 4g

Walnut Ice Cream

Preparation Time: 10 minutes|Servings: 4

Ingredients:

1 cup whole milk
1 tablespoon heavy whipped cream
3 tablespoons smooth walnut paste
1 teaspoon vanilla extract

Preparation:
1. Beat all the ingredients in a bowl until combined. 2. Let the mixture rest for 5 minutes. 3. Transfer the mixture into an empty Ninja CREAMi pint. 4. Cover the pint with the lid and freeze for 24 hours. 5. After 24 hours, remove the lid and place the pint into the outer bowl of the Ninja CREAMi. 6. Install the Creamerizer Paddle onto the lid of the outer bowl. 7. Rotate the lid clockwise to lock. 8. Turn the unit on. 9. Press the ICE CREAM button. 10. When the program is complete, turn the outer bowl and release it from the unit. 11. Serve in bowls.

Serving Suggestions: Top with chopped nuts.
Variation Tip: You can also use skim milk.
Nutritional Information per Serving: Calories: 90|Fat: 8g|Sat Fat: 3g|Carbohydrates: 8g |Fiber: 0g|Sugar: 5g|Protein: 2g

Fruit Carrot Ice Cream

Preparation Time: 15 minutes|Servings: 4

Ingredients:

¾ cup heavy cream
½ cup milk
⅓ cup orange juice
¾ cup sugar
¼ cup frozen carrots
¼ cup pineapple chunks

Preparation:
1. In a bowl, add the heavy cream, milk, orange juice and sugar and beat until sugar is dissolved. 2. In an empty Ninja CREAMi pint container, place the carrots and pineapple chunks and top with milk mixture. 3. Cover the container with storage lid and freeze for 24 hours. 4. After 24 hours, remove the lid from container and arrange into the Outer Bowl of Ninja CREAMi. 5. Install the Creamerizer Paddle onto the lid of Outer Bowl. 6. Then rotate the lid clockwise to lock. 7. Press Power button to turn on the unit. 8. Then press Ice Cream button. 9. When the program is completed, turn the Outer Bowl and release it from the machine. 10. Transfer the ice cream into serving bowls and serve immediately.

Serving Suggestions: Serve with the garnishing of orange zest.
Variation Tip: For best result, use fresh pineapple.
Nutritional Information per Serving: Calories: 250|Fat: 9g|Sat Fat: 5.6g|Carbohydrates: 43.5g|Fiber: 0.3g|Sugar: 41.8g|Protein: 1.7g

Creamy Matcha Ice Cream

Preparation Time: 15 minutes|Servings: 2

Ingredients:

½ tablespoon cream cheese, softened
1 tablespoon matcha powder
1/6 cup granulated sugar
½ teaspoon vanilla extract
⅜ cup heavy cream
½ cup whole milk

Preparation:
1. Microwave the cream cheese for 10 seconds in a large microwave-safe bowl. 2. Combine the matcha powder, sugar, and vanilla extract in a mixing bowl and whisk together for about 60 seconds. 3. Whisk them slowly in the heavy cream and milk until smooth, and the sugar has dissolved. 4. Transfer the mixture into an empty Ninja Creami pint. 5. Cover the container with a pint lid and freeze for 24 hours. 6. After 24 hours, remove the lid from the container and arrange it into the outer bowl of Ninja Creami. 7. Install the "Creamerizer Paddle" onto the lid of the outer bowl. 8. Then rotate the lid clockwise to lock. 9. Turn on the unit. 10. Then select "ICE CREAM" function. 11. When the program is completed, turn the outer bowl and release it from the machine. 12. Serve in bowls.

Serving Suggestions: Top with mint leaves.
Variation Tip: You can use coconut milk.
Nutritional Information per Serving: Calories: 189|Fat: 11g| Sat Fat: 6.9g| Carbohydrates: 20g| Fiber: 0.1g| Sugar: 20g| Protein: 2.6g

Vegan Lemon Vanilla Ice Cream

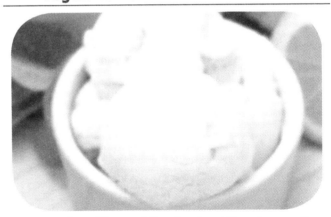

Preparation Time: 10 minutes|Servings: 4

Ingredients:

1 can (14-ounce) full-fat unsweetened coconut milk
½ cup granulated sugar
1 teaspoon vanilla extract
1 teaspoon lemon extract

Preparation:
1. Whisk the coconut milk until it's completely smooth in a medium mixing bowl. Add in the remaining ingredients until everything is well combined and the sugar has dissolved. 2. Transfer the mixture to a Ninja CREAMi Pint. 3. Snap the lid on the pint and freeze it for 24 hours. 4. Remove the lid and assemble the unit as per the user instructions. 5. Select the ICE CREAM program. 6. When the program is complete, remove the outer bowl. 7. Serve in bowls.

Serving Suggestions: Top with sprinkles.
Variation Tip: You can also use stevia instead of sugar.
Nutritional Information per Serving: Calories: 97|Fat: 0.1g|Sat Fat: 0.1g|Carbohydrates: 25g |Fiber: 0g|Sugar: 25g|Protein: 0g

Orange and Pineapple Ice Cream

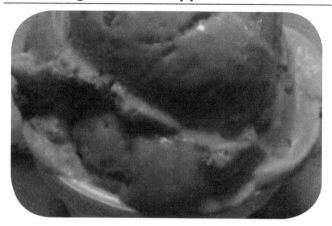

Preparation Time: 5 minutes|Servings: 4

Ingredients:

½ cup milk
¾ cup heavy cream
⅓ cup orange juice

¾ cup sugar
¼ cup frozen carrots
¼ cup pineapple chunks

Preparation:

1. Add the milk, heavy cream, orange juice, and sugar to a medium-sized bowl. Slowly mix until everything is thoroughly combined, and the sugar is dissolved. 2. Put the frozen carrots and pineapple chunks in the Ninja CREAMi Pint. 3. Add the cream mixture. 4. Snap the lid on the pint and freeze it for 24 hours. 5. Remove the lid and assemble the unit as per the user instructions. 6. Select the ICE CREAM program. 7. When the program is complete, remove the outer bowl. 8. Serve in bowls

Serving Suggestions: Top with pineapple chunks.
Variation Tip: You can use any milk.
Nutritional Information per Serving: Calories: 251|Fat: 9g|Sat Fat: 5g|Carbohydrates: 43g |Fiber: 0.4g|Sugar: 42g|Protein: 1.7g

Frozen Hot Chocolate Ice Cream

Preparation Time: 5 minutes|Servings: 4

Ingredients:

1½ cups unsweetened soy milk
2 packets (1½ ounces each) vegan

hot chocolate mix
1 tablespoon raw agave nectar

Preparation:

1. In a bowl, whisk all the ingredients until combined. 2. Transfer the mixture to the Ninja CREAMi Pint. 3. Snap the lid on the pint and freeze it for 24 hours. 4. Remove the lid and assemble the unit as per the user instructions. 5. Press the ICE CREAM program. 6. When the program is complete, remove the outer bowl. 7. Serve in bowls.

Serving Suggestions: Top with marshmallows.
Variation Tip: You can use whole milk.

Nutritional Information per Serving: Calories: 92|Fat: 2g|Sat Fat: 0.4g|Carbohydrates: 14g |Fiber: 0.6g|Sugar: 11g|Protein: 3.8g

Pumpkin Ice Cream

Preparation Time: 20 minutes|Servings: 4

Ingredients:

2 cups butternut squash, cut into 1-inch cubes
1 cup unsweetened oat milk

¾ cup unsweetened coconut cream
2 tablespoons pumpkin pie spice
3 tablespoons maple syrup

Preparation:

1. In a small saucepan over medium-high heat, whisk together all of the ingredients until thoroughly combined. Cook for 10 to 15 minutes, or until the butternut squash is fork-tender. 2. Remove the mixture from the heat and pour it into a blender. Blend for about 60 seconds or until smooth. 3. Let the mixture cool, then transfer it to the Ninja CREAMi Pint. 4. Snap the lid on the pint and freeze it for 24 hours. 5. Remove the lid and assemble the unit as per the user instructions. 6. Select the ICE CREAM program. 7. When the program is complete, remove the outer bowl. 8. Serve in bowls.

Serving Suggestions: Top with chocolate chips.
Variation Tip: You can replace coconut cream with heavy cream.
Nutritional Information per Serving: Calories: 279|Fat: 9.5g|Sat Fat: 8.8g|Carbohydrates: 49g |Fiber: 1.9g|Sugar: 39g|Protein: 1.5g

Vanilla Coconut Ice Cream

Preparation Time: 10 minutes|Servings: 4

Ingredients:

1 can (14-ounce) full-fat unsweetened coconut milk

½ cup granulated sugar
1 teaspoon vanilla extract

Preparation:

1. Whisk the coconut milk until smooth in a medium mixing bowl. Then mix in the remaining ingredients until they're fully incorporated, and the sugar has dissolved. 2. Transfer the mixture to the Ninja CREAMi Pint. 3. Snap the lid on the pint and freeze it for 24 hours. 4. Remove the lid and assemble the unit as per the user instructions. 5. Select the ICE CREAM program. 6. When the program is complete, remove the outer bowl. 7. Serve in bowls.

Serving Suggestions: Top with shredded coconut.
Variation Tip: You can also use stevia instead of sugar.
Nutritional Information per Serving: Calories: 97|Fat: 0.1g|Sat Fat: 35g|Carbohydrates: 25g |Fiber: 0g|Sugar: 25g|Protein: 0g

Peanut Butter Banana Ice Cream

Preparation Time: 5 minutes|Servings: 2

Ingredients:

1 tablespoon cream cheese
¾ tablespoon cocoa powder
½ teaspoon stevia
1 ¼ tablespoons raw agave nectar
½ teaspoon banana extract
⅜ cup coconut cream
½ cup almond milk
1 tablespoon peanut butter
½ banana (fresh)

Preparation:
1. Microwave the cream cheese for 10 seconds in a microwave-safe bowl. 2. Add the cream cheese and the remaining ingredients in a blender and blend until smooth. 3. Transfer the mixture into an empty Ninja Creami pint. 4. Cover the container with a pint lid and freeze for 24 hours. 5. After 24 hours, remove the lid from the container and arrange it into the outer bowl of Ninja Creami. 6. Install the "Creamerizer Paddle" onto the lid of the outer bowl. 7. Then rotate the lid clockwise to lock. 8. Turn on the unit. 9. Then select the "ICE CREAM" function. 10. When the program is completed, turn the outer bowl and release it from the machine. 11. Serve in bowls.

Serving Suggestions: Top with banana slices.
Variation Tip: You can use sugar instead of stevia.
Nutritional Information per Serving: Calories: 1201|Fat: 93g| Sat Fat: 65g| Carbohydrates: 92g| Fiber: 12g| Sugar: 54g| Protein: 20g

Cappuccino Ice Cream

Preparation Time: 10 minutes|Servings: 4

Ingredients:

¾ cup coconut cream
½ cup sugar, granulated
1½ tablespoons cappuccino coffee
powder
1 cup rice milk
1 teaspoon vanilla extract

Preparation:
1. Beat the coconut cream in a bowl until smooth. 2. Add all the remaining ingredients and beat until smooth. 3. Transfer the mixture into an empty Ninja CREAMi Pint. 4. Cover the pint with the lid and freeze for 24 hours. 5. After 24 hours, remove the lid and place the pint into the outer bowl of the Ninja CREAMi. 6. Install the Creamerizer Paddle onto the lid of the outer bowl, then rotate the lid clockwise to lock. 7. Turn the unit on. 8. Press the ICE CREAM button. 9. When the program is complete, turn the outer bowl and release it from the machine. 10. Serve in bowls.

Serving Suggestions: Top with whipped cream.
Variation Tip: You can also use almond milk.
Nutritional Information per Serving: Calories: 230|Fat: 11.2g|Sat Fat: 9.6g|Carbohydrates: 33.8g|Fiber: 1g|Sugar: 26.6g|Protein: 1.1g

Pea Ice Cream

Preparation Time: 5 minutes|Servings: 4

Ingredients:

¾ cup whole milk
½ cup frozen peas, thawed
¼ cup granulated sugar
3 tablespoons grape jam
2 tablespoons peanut butter
powder
1 teaspoons vanilla extract
Purple gel food coloring to desired color (about 5–7 drops)
½ cup heavy cream

Preparation:
1. In a blender pitcher, combine milk, peas, sugar, grape jam, peanut butter powder, and vanilla extract. 2. Blend them together on high for about 60 seconds or until the mixture is perfectly smooth. If using, blend in the food coloring until it is completely blended. 3. Transfer the mixture into an empty Ninja Creami pint. 4. Cover the container with a pint lid and freeze for 24 hours. 5. After 24 hours, remove the lid from the container and arrange it into the outer bowl of Ninja Creami. 6. Install the "Creamerizer Paddle" onto the lid of the outer bowl. 7. Then rotate the lid clockwise to lock. 8. Turn on the unit. 9. Then select the "ICE CREAM" function. 10. When the program is completed, turn the outer bowl and release it from the machine. 11. Serve in bowls.

Serving Suggestions: Top with roasted nuts.
Variation Tip: You can use fruit sweetener.
Nutritional Information per Serving: Calories: 145|Fat: 8g| Sat Fat: 4g| Carbohydrates: 19g| Fiber: 2.2g| Sugar: 16g| Protein: 6g

Earl Grey Ice Cream

Preparation Time: 25 minutes|Servings: 4

Ingredients:

1 cup whole milk
1 cup heavy cream
5 tablespoons monk fruit

sweetener
3 bags of Earl Grey tea

Preparation:
1. Add milk and cream in a medium pot and combine well. 2. Place the saucepan on the stovetop over medium heat and cook until steam starts to rise. 3. Add the monk fruit sweetener and mix well. 4. Add tea bags, steep for 20 minutes, and then remove. 5. Remove the base from the heat and let it cool. 6. Transfer the mixture into an empty Ninja Creami pint. 7. Cover the container with a pint lid and freeze for 24 hours. 8. After 24 hours, remove the lid from the container and arrange it into the outer bowl of Ninja Creami. 9. Install the "Creamerizer Paddle" onto the lid of the outer bowl. 10. Then rotate the lid clockwise to lock. 11. Turn on the unit. 12. Then select the "ICE CREAM" function. 13. When the program is completed, turn the outer bowl and release it from the machine. 14. Serve in bowls.

Serving Suggestions: Top with chocolate chips.
Variation Tip: You can use sugar instead of fruit sweetener.
Nutritional Information per Serving: Calories: 140|Fat: 13g| Sat Fat: 8g| Carbohydrates: 3.9g| Fiber: 0g| Sugar: 3.2g| Protein: 2g

Brown Sugar Ice Cream

Preparation Time: 15 minutes|Servings: 2

Ingredients:

1 ½ eggs

½ cup unsweetened soy milk

¼ cup unsweetened creamer
⅛ cup packed dark brown sugar
Pinch of kosher salt

⅛ cup granulated sugar
½ tablespoon water

Preparation:
1. Prepare vegan eggs according to the package directions. 2. Whisk the soy milk, creamer, brown sugar, salt, and vegan egg in a medium mixing bowl. 3. Set a medium saucepan over medium heat, combine the granulated sugar and water and cook, occasionally swirling, until the mixture caramelizes, about 5 minutes. 4. When the sugar has caramelized, add the vegan egg mixture in a slow, steady stream, stirring gently to incorporate. 5. Remove the base from the heat and let it cool. 6. Transfer the mixture into an empty Ninja Creami pint. 7. Cover the container with a pint lid and freeze for 24 hours. 8. After 24 hours, remove the lid from the container and arrange it into the outer bowl of Ninja Creami. 9. Install the "Creamerizer Paddle" onto the lid of the outer bowl. 10. Then rotate the lid clockwise to lock. 11. Turn on the unit. 12. Then select the "ICE CREAM" function. 13. When the program is completed, turn the outer bowl and release it from the machine. 14. Serve in bowls.

Serving Suggestions: Sprinkle brown sugar on top.
Variation Tip: You can use any milk.
Nutritional Information per Serving: Calories: 140|Fat: 4g| Sat Fat: 0.1g| Carbohydrates: 34g| Fiber: 3g| Sugar: 28g| Protein: 4g

Lavender Ice Cream

Preparation Time: 20 minutes|Servings: 2

Ingredients:

½ cup whole milk
½ cup heavy cream
1 tablespoon dried lavender
1 tablespoon honey

3 tablespoons monk fruit
sweetener
1/16 teaspoon salt

Preparation:
1. Combine milk and heavy cream in a medium saucepan. 2. Cook, occasionally stirring, until wisps of steam appear in the pot over medium heat. 3. Allow 20 minutes for the lavender to steep. 4. Remove the pot from the heat and drain the base into a medium bowl through a fine-mesh strainer. 5. Whisk the honey, monk fruit sweetener, and salt in a mixing bowl. 6. Transfer the mixture into an empty Ninja Creami pint. 7. Cover the container with a pint lid and freeze for 24 hours. 8. After 24 hours, remove the lid from the container and arrange it into the outer bowl of Ninja Creami. 9. Install the "Creamerizer Paddle" onto the lid of the outer bowl. 10. Then rotate the lid clockwise to lock. 11. Turn on the unit. 12. Then select the "ICE CREAM" function. 13. When the program is completed, turn the outer bowl and release it from the machine. 14. Serve in bowls.

Serving Suggestions: Top with nuts.
Variation Tip: You can use sugar instead of fruit sweetener.
Nutritional Information per Serving: Calories: 231|Fat: 16g| Sat Fat: 8g| Carbohydrates: 19g| Fiber: 1g| Sugar: 16g| Protein: 4g

Coconut Coffee Ice Cream

Preparation Time: 5 minutes|Servings: 2

Ingredients:

⅜ cup unsweetened coconut cream
¼ cup granulated sugar
¾ tablespoon coffee
½ cup milk
½ teaspoon vanilla extract

Preparation:

1. Whisk the unsweetened coconut cream until smooth in a large mixing bowl. 2. Whisk in the remaining ingredients until completely blended, and the sugar is dissolved. 3. Transfer the mixture into an empty Ninja Creami pint. 4. Cover the container with a pint lid and freeze for 24 hours. 5. After 24 hours, remove the lid from the container and arrange it into the outer bowl of Ninja Creami. 6. Install the "Creamerizer Paddle" onto the lid of the outer bowl. 7. Then rotate the lid clockwise to lock. 8. Turn on the unit. 9. Then select the "ICE CREAM" function. 10. When the program is completed, turn the outer bowl and release it from the machine. 11. Serve in bowls.

Serving Suggestions: Top with nuts.
Variation Tip: You can use coconut milk.
Nutritional Information per Serving: Calories: 427|Fat: 30g| Sat Fat: 24g| Carbohydrates: 41g| Fiber: 0.5g| Sugar: 25g| Protein: 3.4g

Cream Cheese Ice Cream

Preparation Time: 10 minutes|Servings: 4

Ingredients:

1 tablespoon cream cheese, softened
⅓ cup sugar
1 teaspoon vanilla extract
¾ cup heavy cream
1 cup whole milk

Preparation:

1. Microwave cream cheese for 10 seconds in a large microwave-safe bowl. 2. Combine the sugar and orange extract in a mixing bowl with a whisk for about 60 seconds. 3. Whisk slowly in the heavy cream and milk until smooth, and the sugar has dissolved. 4. Transfer the mixture into an empty Ninja Creami pint. 5. Cover the container with a pint lid and freeze for 24 hours. 6. After 24 hours, remove the lid from the container and arrange it into the outer bowl of Ninja Creami. 7. Install the "Creamerizer Paddle" onto the lid of the outer bowl. 8. Then rotate the lid clockwise to lock. 9. Turn on the unit. 10. Then select the "ICE CREAM" function. 11. When the program is completed, turn the outer bowl and release it from the machine. 12. Serve in bowls.

Serving Suggestions: Top with orange zest.
Variation Tip: You can add fresh orange.
Nutritional Information per Serving: Calories: 188|Fat: 11g| Sat Fat: 6g| Carbohydrates: 20g| Fiber: 0g| Sugar: 20g| Protein: 2g

Banana Apple pie Ice Cream

Preparation Time: 7 minutes|Servings: 2

Ingredients:

1 banana, ripe, mashed
⅛ cup sugar
¼ teaspoon apple pie spice mix
¾ cups milk of choice

Preparation:

1. Combine all ingredients in a blender and blend on high until smooth. 2. Transfer the mixture into an empty Ninja Creami pint. 3. Cover the container with a pint lid and freeze for 24 hours. 4. After 24 hours, remove the lid from the container and arrange it into the outer bowl of Ninja Creami. 5. Install the "Creamerizer Paddle" onto the lid of the outer bowl. 6. Then rotate the lid clockwise to lock. 7. Turn on the unit. 8. Then select the "ICE CREAM" function. 9. When the program is completed, turn the outer bowl and release it from the machine. 10. Serve in bowls.

Serving Suggestions: Top with chocolate syrup.
Variation Tip: You can use any milk.
Nutritional Information per Serving: Calories: 113|Fat: 0.2g| Sat Fat: 0.1g| Carbohydrates: 29g| Fiber: 1.5g| Sugar: 18g| Protein: 0.7g

Banana Chocolate Ice Cream

Preparation Time: 10 minutes|Servings: 4

Ingredients:

1 tablespoon (½ ounce) cream cheese, softened
⅓ cup granulated sugar
1 teaspoon banana extract
¾ cup heavy cream
1 cup whole milk
2 tablespoons chocolate syrup

Preparation:

1. Microwave the cream cheese for 10 seconds in a large microwave-safe bowl. 2. Combine the sugar, chocolate syrup, and banana extract in a mixing bowl with a whisk for about 60 seconds. 3. Whisk slowly in the heavy cream and milk until smooth, and the sugar has dissolved. 4. Transfer the mixture into an empty Ninja Creami pint. 5. Cover the container with a pint lid and freeze for 24 hours. 6. After 24 hours, remove the lid from the container and arrange it into the outer bowl of Ninja Creami. 7. Install the "Creamerizer Paddle" onto the lid of the outer bowl. 8. Then rotate the lid clockwise to lock. 9. Turn on the unit. 10. Then select the "ICE CREAM" function. 11. When the program is completed, turn the outer bowl and release it from the machine. 12. Serve in bowls.

Serving Suggestions: Top with chocolate syrup.
Variation Tip: You can add fresh banana.
Nutritional Information per Serving: Calories: 215|Fat: 11g| Sat Fat: 6g| Carbohydrates: 26g| Fiber: 0.2g| Sugar: 24g| Protein: 2.8g

Gingersnap Ice Cream

Preparation Time: 10 minutes|Servings: 4

Ingredients:

2 cups oat milk
⅓ cup packed brown sugar
2 teaspoons ground cinnamon
1½ teaspoons ground ginger
½ teaspoon ground cloves

Preparation:

1. Mix all the ingredients in a small saucepan and stir to combine. 2. Cook for 5 minutes over medium heat or until the sugar dissolves. 3. Remove the mixture from the heat and transfer it to the Ninja CREAMi Pint. 4. Snap the lid on the pint and freeze it for 24 hours. 5. Remove the lid and assemble the unit as per the user instructions. 6. Select the ICE CREAM program. 7. When the program is complete, remove the outer bowl. 8. Serve in bowls.

Serving Suggestions: Garnish with ground cinnamon on top.
Variation Tip: You can use either dark or light packed brown sugar.
Nutritional Information per Serving: Calories: 117|Fat: 1g|Sat Fat: 0g|Carbohydrates: 25g |Fiber: 1.8g|Sugar: 21g|Protein: 2g

Chocolate Broccoli Ice Cream

Preparation Time: 5 minutes|Servings: 2

Ingredients:

¼ cup frozen broccoli florets, thawed
¼ cup sugar
½ cup whole milk
1 ½ tablespoons cocoa powder
1/6 cup heavy cream

Preparation:

1. Combine broccoli, sugar, milk, and cocoa powder in a blender pitcher. 2. Blend them together on high for 60 seconds or until the mixture is perfectly smooth. 3. Transfer the mixture into an empty Ninja Creami pint. 4. Stir in the heavy cream mix until everything is fully mixed. 5. Cover the container with a pint lid and freeze for 24 hours. 6. After 24 hours, remove the lid from the container and arrange it into the outer bowl of Ninja Creami. 7. Install the "Creamerizer Paddle" onto the lid of the outer bowl. 8. Then rotate the lid clockwise to lock. 9. Turn on the unit. 10. Then select the "ICE CREAM" function. 11. When the program is completed, turn the outer bowl and release it from the machine. 12. Serve in bowls.

Serving Suggestions: Top with almonds and marshmallows.
Variation Tip: You can also add chocolate extract.
Nutritional Information per Serving: Calories: 144|Fat: 5g| Sat Fat: 3g| Carbohydrates: 21g| Fiber: 0.4g| Sugar: 21g| Protein: 2g

Matcha Ice Cream

Preparation Time: 15 minutes|Cooking Time: 10 seconds|Servings: 4

Ingredients:

1 tablespoon cream cheese, softened
⅓ cup granulated sugar
2 tablespoons matcha powder
1 teaspoon vanilla extract
1 cup whole milk
¾ cup heavy cream

Preparation:
1. In a large microwave-safe bowl, add the cream cheese and microwave for on High for about ten seconds. 2. Remove from the microwave and stir until smooth. 3. Add the sugar, matcha powder and vanilla extract and with a wire whisk, beat until the mixture looks like frosting. 4. Slowly add the milk and heavy cream and beat until well combined. 5. Transfer the mixture into an empty Ninja CREAMi pint container. 6. Cover the container with storage lid and freeze for 24 hours. 7. After 24 hours, remove the lid from container and arrange into the Outer Bowl of Ninja CREAMi. 8. Install the Creamerizer Paddle onto the lid of Outer Bowl. 9. Then rotate the lid clockwise to lock. 10. Press Power button to turn on the unit. 11. Then press Ice Cream button. 12. When the program is completed, turn the Outer Bowl and release it from the machine. 13. Transfer the ice cream into serving bowls and serve immediately.

Serving Suggestions: Serve with the topping of chopped nuts.
Variation Tip: You can use almond extract instead of vanilla extract.
Nutritional Information per Serving: Calories: 188|Fat: 11.2g|Sat Fat: 6.9g|Carbohydrates: 20.3g|Fiber: 0g|Sugar: 20g|Protein: 2.6g

Coffee Ice Cream

Preparation Time: 10 minutes|Servings: 2

Ingredients:

½ cup whole milk
1 tablespoon finely ground coffee
½ cup cream
1 tablespoon agave nectar
3 tablespoons sugar
½ teaspoon vanilla extract

Preparation:
1. Pour milk into a medium pot. 2. Bring to a simmer in a pot on the stove over medium heat. 3. Steep for 1 minute after adding the coffee. 4. Combine cream, ground coffee, coffee liqueur, agave nectar, monk fruit sweetener, and vanilla extract to make the base. Let it cool. 5. Transfer the mixture into an empty Ninja Creami pint. 6. Cover the container with a pint lid and freeze for 24 hours. 7. After 24 hours, remove the lid from the container and arrange it into the outer bowl of Ninja Creami. 8. Install the "Creamerizer Paddle" onto the lid of the outer bowl. 9. Then rotate the lid clockwise to lock. 10. Turn on the unit. 11. Then select the "ICE CREAM" function. 12. When the program is completed, turn the outer bowl and release it from the machine. 13. Serve in bowls.

Serving Suggestions: Top with nuts.
Variation Tip: You can use any fruit sweetener.
Nutritional Information per Serving: Calories: 93|Fat: 5g| Sat Fat: 3g| Carbohydrates: 7g| Fiber: 0g| Sugar: 6g| Protein: 2g

Green Tea Ice Cream

Preparation Time: 10 minutes|Servings: 4

Ingredients:

⅓ cup granulated sugar
1 tablespoon cream cheese
2 tablespoons vanilla extract
1½ tablespoons green tea (matcha)
powder
1 cup milk
¾ cup heavy cream

Preparation:
1. Microwave the cream cheese for 10 seconds and mix until smooth. 2. Mix the softened cream cheese, sugar, green tea powder, and vanilla extract in a bowl and beat well. 3. Add the milk and cream into the mixture. 4. Transfer the mixture into an empty Ninja CREAMi Pint. 5. Cover the container with the lid and freeze for 24 hours. 6. After 24 hours, remove the lid and place the pint in the outer bowl of the Ninja CREAMi. 7. Install the Creamerizer Paddle and then lock the lid. Turn the unit on. 8. Press the ICE CREAM button. 9. When the program is complete, turn the outer bowl and release it from the unit. 10. Serve in bowls.

Serving Suggestions: Top with some chopped nuts.
Variation Tip: You can also use whipping cream.
Nutritional Information per Serving: Calories: 188|Fat: 11.2g|Sat Fat: 6.9g|Carbohydrates: 20.3g |Fiber: 0g|Sugar: 20g|Protein: 2.6g

Strawberry Shortcake Milkshake

Preparation Time: 2 minutes|Servings: 2

Ingredients:

1½ cups strawberry ice cream
½ cup whole milk
¼ premade pound cake, crumbled
¼ cup fresh strawberries, trimmed, cut in quarters

Preparation:
1. Fill an empty CREAMi Pint with the ice cream. 2. Create a 1-inch wide hole in the bottom of the pint using a spoon. Fill the hole with the remaining ingredients. 3. Arrange the container into the outer bowl of the Ninja CREAMi. 4. Install the Creamerizer Paddle onto the lid of the outer bowl, then rotate the lid clockwise to lock. 5. Turn the unit on. 6. Press the MILKSHAKE button. 7. When the program is complete, turn the outer bowl and release it from the machine. 8. Transfer the shake into serving glasses and serve immediately.

Serving Suggestions: Serve with a garnishing of fresh berries.
Variation Tip: You can use any milk you prefer.
Nutritional Information per Serving: Calories: 347 | Fat: 14g | Sat Fat: 4g | Carbohydrates: 34g | Fiber: 0.9g | Sugar: 13g | Protein: 5g

Vanilla Banana Milkshake

Preparation Time: 10 minutes|Servings: 2

Ingredients:

1 scoop vanilla ice cream
2 small bananas, peeled and halved
7 fluid ounces semi-skimmed milk

Preparation:
1. In an empty Ninja CREAMi pint container, place ice cream followed by bananas and milk. 2. Arrange the container into the Outer Bowl of Ninja CREAMi. 3. Install the Creamerizer Paddle onto the lid of Outer Bowl. 4. Then rotate the lid clockwise to lock. 5. Press Power button to turn on the unit. 6. Then press Milkshake button. 7. When the program is completed, turn the Outer Bowl and release it from the machine. 8. Transfer the shake into serving glasses and serve immediately.

Serving Suggestions: Serve with the sprinkling of ground cinnamon.
Variation Tip: You can use non-dairy milk in this recipe.
Nutritional Information per Serving: Calories: 210 | Fat: 4.9g|Sat Fat: 2.4g|Carbohydrates: 36.3g|Fiber: 2.9g|Sugar: 19.4g|Protein: 5.4g

Peanut Butter Milkshake

Preparation Time: 10 minutes|Servings: 2

Ingredients:

½ cup canned cashew milk
1½ cups vanilla ice cream
¼ cup peanut butter

Preparation:
1. Put the vanilla ice cream in the Ninja CREAMi Pint. 2. With a spoon, create a 1½-inch wide hole in the center that reaches the bottom of the pint. 3. Add the peanut butter and cashew milk into the hole. 4. Assemble the unit as per the user instructions. 5. Select the MILKSHAKE program. 6. When the program is complete, remove the outer bowl. 7. Transfer the shake into serving glasses and serve immediately.

Serving Suggestions: Serve with the topping of whipped cream.
Variation Tip: You can also use coconut ice cream.
Nutritional Information per Serving: Calories: 298 | Fat: 22g | Sat Fat: 6.8g | Carbohydrates: 18.6g |Fiber: 2.3g | Sugar: 13.5g | Protein: 9.8g

Marshmallow Milkshake

Preparation Time: 10 minutes|Servings: 2

Ingredients:

1½ cups vanilla ice cream
½ cup oat milk
½ cup marshmallow cereal

Preparation:

1. In an empty Ninja CREAMi pint container, place ice cream followed by oat milk and marshmallow cereal. 2. Arrange the container into the Outer Bowl of Ninja CREAMi. 3. Install the Creamerizer Paddle onto the lid of Outer Bowl. 4. Then rotate the lid clockwise to lock. 5. Press Power button to turn on the unit. 6. Then press Milkshake button. 7. When the program is completed, turn the Outer Bowl and release it from the machine. 8. Transfer the shake into serving glasses and serve immediately.

Serving Suggestions: Serve with the topping of mini marshmallows.
Variation Tip: Feel free to use milk of your choice.
Nutritional Information per Serving: Calories: 165 | Fat: 6.1g|Sat Fat: 3.5g|Carbohydrates: 24.8g| Fiber: 1.1g|Sugar: 19.3g|Protein: 3g

Salted Caramel Pretzel Milkshake

Preparation Time: 2 minutes|Servings: 2

Ingredients:

1½ cups vanilla ice cream
½ cup whole milk
2 tablespoons caramel sauce
⅓ cup pretzels, broken
2 pinches sea salt

Preparation:

1. Fill an empty CREAMi Pint with the ice cream. 2. Create a 1-inch wide hole in the bottom of the pint using a spoon. Fill the hole with the remaining ingredients. 3. Arrange the pint into the outer bowl of the Ninja CREAMi. 4. Install the Creamerizer Paddle onto the lid of the outer bowl, then rotate the lid clockwise to lock. 5. Turn on the unit. 6. Press the MILKSHAKE button. 7. When the program is complete, turn the outer bowl and release it from the machine. 8. Transfer the shake into serving glasses and serve immediately.

Serving Suggestions: Garnish with more crushed pretzels and sea salt.
Variation Tip: You can use vanilla vodka instead of milk.
Nutritional Information per Serving: Calories: 193 | Fat: 7g | Sat Fat: 4g | Carbohydrates: 23g | Fiber: 0.5g | Sugar: 13g | Protein: 4g

Mocha Banana Milkshake

Preparation Time: 2 minutes|Servings: 2

Ingredients:

1½ cups vegan chocolate ice cream
½ cup cashew milk
½ cup fresh ripe banana
1 tablespoon instant coffee powder

Preparation:

1. Fill an empty CREAMi Pint with the ice cream. 2. Create a 1½-inch wide hole in the bottom of the pint using a spoon. Fill the hole with the remaining ingredients. 3. Place the pint into the outer bowl of the Ninja CREAMi. 4. Install the Creamerizer Paddle onto the lid of the outer bowl, then rotate the lid clockwise to lock. 5. Turn on the unit. 6. Press the MILKSHAKE button. 7. When the program is complete, turn the outer bowl and release it from the machine. 8. Transfer the shake into serving glasses and serve immediately.

Serving Suggestions: Serve with a sprinkling of ground cinnamon.
Variation Tip: You can use any milk of your choice.
Nutritional Information per Serving: Calories: 142 | Fat: 5.9g | Sat Fat: 3.4g | Carbohydrates: 20g | Fiber: 1g | Sugar: 15g | Protein: 2g

Chocolate Hazelnut Milkshake

Preparation Time: 2 Minutes | Cook Time: 10 Minutes | Serves: 2

Ingredients:

1 cup chocolate ice cream
½ cup whole milk

¼ cup hazelnut spread

Preparation:

1. Place the ice cream in an empty CREAMi Pint. 2. Create a 1½-inch-wide hole in the bottom of the Pint using a spoon. Fill the hole with the remaining ingredients. 3. Place Pint in outer bowl, install Creamerizer Paddle onto outer bowl lid and lock the lid assembly on the outer bowl. Place bowl assembly on motor base and twist the handle right to raise the platform and lock in place. 4. Select MILKSHAKE. 5. When the milkshake has finished processing, take it from the Pint and serve right away.

Serving Suggestion: Serve immediately.
Variation Tip: Add more nuts if you like.
Nutritional Information per Serving: Calories 516 | Protein 10g | Carbohydrate 70g | Dietary Fiber 0.5g | Sugar 67g | Fat 22g | Sodium 200mg

Mixed Berries Milkshake

Preparation Time: 10 minutes | Servings: 2

Ingredients:

1½ cups vanilla ice cream
½ cup milk

½ cup fresh mixed berries

Preparation:

1. In an empty Ninja CREAMi pint container, place ice cream followed by milk and berries. 2. Arrange the container into the outer bowl of Ninja CREAMi. 3. Install the Creamerizer Paddle onto the lid of Outer Bowl. 4. Then rotate the lid clockwise to lock. 5. Press Power button to turn on the unit. 6. Then press Milkshake button. 7. When the program is completed, turn the Outer Bowl and release it from the machine. 8. Transfer the shake into serving glasses and serve immediately.

Serving Suggestions: Serve with garnishing of fresh berries.
Variation Tip: You can also use strawberry ice cream in this recipe
Nutritional Information per Serving: Calories: 153 | Fat: 6.6g | Sat Fat: 4.1g | Carbohydrates: 19.3g | Fiber: 1.6g | Sugar: 15.8g | Protein: 4g

Amaretto Cookies Milkshake

Preparation Time: 10 minutes | Servings: 2

Ingredients:

½ cup amaretto-flavored coffee creamer
1 cup whole milk
¼ cup amaretto liqueur

¼ cup chocolate chip cookies, chopped
1 tablespoon agave nectar

Preparation:

1. Place all the ingredients except for the cookies in the Ninja CREAMi Pint and stir to combine. 2. Snap the lid on the pint and freeze it for 24 hours. 3. Remove the lid and assemble the unit as per the user instructions. 4. Select the MILKSHAKE program. 5. When the program is complete, create a 1½-inch wide hole in the center that reaches the bottom of the pint container with a spoon. 6. Add the chopped cookies into the hole and select the MIX-IN program. 7. When the program is complete, remove the outer bowl. 8. Transfer the shake into serving glasses and serve immediately.

Serving Suggestions: Serve with a topping of mini chocolate cookies.
Variation Tip: You can use any milk you prefer.
Nutritional Information per Serving: Calories: 371 | Fat: 17.6g | Sat Fat: 9g | Carbohydrates: 25.9g | Fiber: 1g | Sugar: 42.2g | Protein: 6.5g

Pecan Milkshake

Preparation Time: 10 minutes | Servings: 2

Ingredients:

1½ cups vanilla ice cream
½ cup unsweetened soy milk
2 tablespoons maple syrup

¼ cup pecans, chopped
1 teaspoon ground cinnamon
Pinch of salt

Preparation:

1. In an empty Ninja CREAMi pint container, place ice cream followed by soy milk, maple syrup, pecans, cinnamon and salt. 2. Arrange the container into the Outer Bowl of Ninja CREAMi. 3. Install the Creamerizer Paddle onto the lid of Outer Bowl. 4. Then rotate the lid clockwise to lock. 5. Press Power button to turn on the unit. 6. Then press Milkshake button. 7. When the program is completed, turn the Outer Bowl and release it from the machine. 8. Transfer the shake into serving glasses and serve immediately.

Serving Suggestions: Serve with the topping of extra pecans.
Variation Tip: Maple syrup can be replaced with honey.
Nutritional Information per Serving: Calories: 309 | Fat: 18.5g | Sat Fat: 4.7g | Carbohydrates: 32.6g | Fiber: 3.2g | Sugar: 25.5g | Protein: 5.6g

Cashew Butter Milkshake

Preparation Time: 10 minutes|Servings: 2

Ingredients:
1½ cups vanilla ice cream   ¼ cup cashew butter
½ cup canned cashew milk

Preparation:
1. In an empty Ninja CREAMi pint container, place the ice cream. 2. With a spoon, create a 1½-inch wide hole in the center that reaches the bottom of the pint container. 3. Add the remaining ingredients into the hole. 4. Arrange the container into the Outer Bowl of Ninja CREAMi. 5. Install the Creamerizer Paddle onto the lid of Outer Bowl. 6. Then rotate the lid clockwise to lock. 7. Press Power button to turn on the unit. 8. Then press Milkshake button. 9. When the program is completed, turn the Outer Bowl and release it from the machine. 10. Transfer the shake into serving glasses and serve immediately.

Serving Suggestions: Serve with topping of chopped cashews.
Variation Tip: Full-fat coconut milk can be also used instead of cashew milk.
Nutritional Information per Serving: Calories: 297 | Fat: 21.6g|Sat Fat: 6.5g|Carbohydrates: 21.1g|Fiber: 1g|Sugar: 10.5g|Protein: 7.4g

Apple Pie Milkshake

Preparation Time: 2 minutes|Servings: 2

Ingredients:
1½ cups vanilla ice cream   ¼ cup whole milk
2 ounces premade apple pie

Preparation:
1. Fill an empty CREAMi Pint with the ice cream. 2. Create a 1-inch wide hole in the bottom of the pint using a spoon. Fill the hole with the remaining ingredients. 3. Place the pint into the outer bowl of the Ninja CREAMi. 4. Install the Creamerizer Paddle onto the lid of the outer bowl, then rotate the lid clockwise to lock. 5. Turn the unit on. 6. Press the MILKSHAKE button. 7. When the program is complete, turn the outer bowl and release it from the machine. 8. Transfer the shake into serving glasses and serve immediately.

Serving Suggestions: Serve with a sprinkling of ground cinnamon.
Variation Tip: You can use non-dairy milk in this recipe.
Nutritional Information per Serving: Calories: 243 | Fat: 6g | Sat Fat: 4g | Carbohydrates: 33g | Fiber: 5g | Sugar: 32g | Protein: 3g

Brownie Milkshake

Preparation Time: 2 minutes|Servings: 2

Ingredients:
½ cup chocolate ice cream   1¼ cups brownie, chopped into
½ cup whole milk   bite-sized pieces

Preparation:
1. Fill an empty CREAMi Pint with the ice cream. 2. Create a 1-inch wide hole in the bottom of the pint using a spoon. Fill the hole with the remaining ingredients. 3. Place the pint into the outer bowl of the Ninja CREAMi. 4. Install the Creamerizer Paddle onto the lid of the outer bowl, then rotate the lid clockwise to lock. 5. Turn the unit on. 6. Press the MILKSHAKE button. 7. When the program is complete, turn the outer bowl and release it from the machine. 8. Transfer the shake into serving glasses and serve immediately.

Serving Suggestions: Serve with a topping of whipped cream.
Variation Tip: You can also use almond milk.
Nutritional Information per Serving: Calories: 45 | Fat: 2g | Sat Fat: 1.4g | Carbohydrates: 5g | Fiber: 0.2g | Sugar: 4g | Protein: 0.7g

Avocado Milkshake

Preparation Time: 10 minutes | Servings: 2

Ingredients:

1 small ripe avocado, peeled, pitted, and chopped
1 cup coconut ice cream
1 teaspoon fresh lemon juice
1 teaspoon vanilla extract
½ cup oat milk
2 tablespoons agave nectar
Pinch of salt

Preparation:

1. Put the ice cream, followed by the remaining ingredients, in the Ninja CREAMi Pint. 2. Assemble the unit as per the user instructions. 3. Select the MILKSHAKE program. 4. When the program is complete, remove the outer bowl. 5. Transfer the shake into serving glasses and serve immediately.

Serving Suggestions: Serve with a garnishing of chopped pistachios.
Variation Tip: You can also use vanilla ice cream.
Nutritional Information per Serving: Calories: 283 | Fat: 15.2g | Sat Fat: 4g | Carbohydrates: 35.2g |Fiber: 5.6g | Sugar: 27.4g | Protein: 3.3g

Chocolate Cherry Milkshake

Preparation Time: 10 minutes | Servings: 2

Ingredients:

1½ cups chocolate ice cream
½ cup canned cherries in syrup,
drained
¼ cup whole milk

Preparation:

1. In an empty Ninja CREAMi pint container, place ice cream followed by cherries and milk. 2. Arrange the container into the Outer Bowl of Ninja CREAMi. 3. Install the Creamerizer Paddle onto the lid of Outer Bowl. 4. Then rotate the lid clockwise to lock. 5. Press Power button to turn on the unit. 6. Then press Milkshake button. 7. When the program is completed, turn the Outer Bowl and release it from the machine. 8. Transfer the shake into serving glasses and serve immediately.

Serving Suggestions: Serve with the garnishing of mascarpone cherries.
Variation Tip: For best result use canned cherries.
Nutritional Information per Serving: Calories: 143 | Fat: 6.3g|Sat Fat: 4g|Carbohydrates: 18.8g|Fiber: 1.1g|Sugar: 16.7g|Protein: 3.2g

Choco Cream Cheese Milkshake

Preparation Time: 5 minutes | Servings: 2

Ingredients:

1 ½ cup chocolate ice cream
½ cup whole milk
2 tablespoons cream cheese
3 chocolate cookies, crushed

Preparation:

1. In an empty Ninja Creami pint, place all ingredients and mix well. 2. Arrange the container into the outer bowl of Ninja Creami. 3. Install the "Creamerizer Paddle" onto the lid of the outer bowl. 4. Then rotate the lid clockwise to lock. 5. Turn on the unit. 6. Then select the "MILKSHAKE" function. 7. When the program is completed, turn the outer bowl and release it from the machine. 8. Transfer the shake into serving glasses and serve immediately.

Serving Suggestions: Garnish with extra cookies.
Variation Tip: You can skip the cheese.
Nutritional Information per Serving: Calories: 307 | Fat: 15g| Sat Fat: 7.4g| Carbohydrates: 38g| Fiber: 1.3g| Sugar: 23g| Protein: 4.7g

Cacao Mint Milkshake

Preparation Time: 10 minutes | Servings: 2

Ingredients:

1½ cups vanilla ice cream
½ cup canned full-fat coconut milk
1 teaspoon matcha powder
¼ cup cacao nibs
1 teaspoon peppermint extract

Preparation:

1. In an empty Ninja CREAMi pint container, place ice cream followed by coconut milk, matcha powder, cacao nibs and peppermint extract. 2. Arrange the container into the Outer Bowl of Ninja CREAMi. 3. Install the Creamerizer Paddle onto the lid of Outer Bowl. 4. Then rotate the lid clockwise to lock. 5. Press Power button to turn on the unit. 6. Then press Milkshake button. 7. When the program is completed, turn the Outer Bowl and release it from the machine. 8. Transfer the shake into serving glasses and serve immediately.

Serving Suggestions: Serve with the topping crushed chocolate cookies.
Variation Tip: use high quality cacao nibs.
Nutritional Information per Serving: Calories: 363 | Fat: 26.2g|Sat Fat: 19.7g|Carbohydrates: 26.8g|Fiber: 4.8g|Sugar: 19.8g|Protein: 5.4g

Almond Matcha Milkshake

Preparation Time: 10 minutes|Servings: 2

Ingredients:
1½ cups vanilla ice cream
½ cup almond milk
1 teaspoon matcha powder
¼ teaspoon vanilla extract

Preparation:
1. Put the ice cream in the Ninja CREAMi Pint, followed by the almond milk, matcha powder, and vanilla extract. 2. Assemble the unit as per the user instructions. 3. Select the MILKSHAKE program. 4. When the program is complete, remove the outer bowl. 5. Transfer the shake into serving glasses and serve immediately.

Serving Suggestions: Serve with a topping of whipped fresh cream.
Variation Tip: You can use any milk of your choice.
Nutritional Information per Serving: Calories: 252 | Fat: 19.6g | Sat Fat: 16.1g | Carbohydrates: 17.9g | Fiber: 2.7g | Sugar: 13.1g | Protein: 3.1g

Marshmallow Milkshake

Preparation Time: 5 minutes|Servings: 2

Ingredients:
1 ½ cups vanilla ice cream
½ cup whole milk
½ cup marshmallow cereal

Preparation:
1. In an empty Ninja Creami pint, place all ingredients and mix well. 2. Arrange the container into the outer bowl of Ninja Creami. 3. Install the "Creamerizer Paddle" onto the lid of the outer bowl. 4. Then rotate the lid clockwise to lock. 5. Turn on the unit. 6. Then select the "MILKSHAKE" function. 7. When the program is completed, turn the outer bowl and release it from the machine. 8. Transfer the shake into serving glasses and serve immediately.

Serving Suggestions: Garnish with sprinkles.
Variation Tip: You can use oat milk.
Nutritional Information per Serving: Calories: 270 | Fat: 17g| Sat Fat: 4g| Carbohydrates: 23g| Fiber: 3g| Sugar: 12g| Protein: 5g

Orange Milkshake

Preparation Time: 2 Minutes|Cook Time: 5 Minutes|Serves: 1

Ingredients:
1 cup orange juice
2 scoops vanilla ice cream
½ cup milk
2 teaspoons white sugar

Preparation:
1. Place orange juice, ice cream, milk, and sugar in an empty CREAMi Pint. 2. Place Pint in outer bowl, install Creamerizer Paddle onto outer bowl lid and lock the lid assembly on the outer bowl. Place the bowl assembly on the motor base and crank the lever to elevate and secure the platform in place. 3. Select MILKSHAKE. 4. Remove the milkshake from the Pint after the processing is finished.

Serving Suggestion: Serve cold.
Variation Tip: Add nuts of your choice.
Nutritional Information per Serving: Calories 346 | Protein 8g | Carbohydrate 62g | Dietary Fiber 1g | Sugar 52g | Fat 7.8g | Sodium 87.3mg

Apple Milkshake

Preparation Time: 10 minutes|Servings: 2

Ingredients:
1 cup vanilla ice cream
½ cup apples, peeled and chopped
1½ cups semi-skimmed milk

Preparation:
1. Put the vanilla ice cream, followed by the apples and milk, in the Ninja CREAMi Pint. 2. Assemble the unit as per the user instructions. 3. Select the MILKSHAKE program. 4. When the program is complete, remove the outer bowl. 5. Transfer the shake into serving glasses and serve immediately.

Serving Suggestions: Serve topped with mint leaves and apple chunks.
Variation Tip: You can use non-dairy milk in this recipe.
Nutritional Information per Serving: Calories: 186 | Fat: 5.4g | Sat Fat: 2.3g | Carbohydrates: 24.7g |Fiber: 1.6g | Sugar: 12.8g | Protein: 6.7g

Dulce De Leche Milkshake

Preparation Time: 5 Minutes|Cook Time: 5 Minutes|Serves: 2

Ingredients:

1 cup vanilla or coffee ice cream
½ cup milk
2 tablespoons sweetened

condensed milk
¼ teaspoon salt

Preparation:

1. Place all ingredients into an empty CREAMi Pint. 2. Place Pint in outer bowl, install Creamerizer Paddle onto outer bowl lid and lock the lid assembly on the outer bowl. Place the bowl assembly on the motor base and crank the lever to elevate and secure the platform in place. 3. Choose the MILKSHAKE option. 4. Remove the milkshake from the Pint after the function is finished.

Serving Suggestion: Serve with a topping of whipped cream.
Variation Tip: You can top the shake with chocolate or honey if desired.
Nutritional Information per Serving: Calories 276 | Protein 7g | Carbohydrate 48g | Dietary Fiber 0.5g | Sugar 39g | Fat 6g | Sodium 530mg

Peanut Butter and Jelly Milkshake

Preparation Time: 3 Minutes|Cook Time: 5 Minutes|Serves: 2

Ingredients:

3 tablespoons peanut butter
3 tablespoons grape jelly
1 cup milk

5 ice cubes
½ teaspoon vanilla extract

Preparation:

1. Add the milk, peanut butter, ice cubes, vanilla extract, and grape jelly into an empty CREAMi Pint. 2. Place the Pint in the outer bowl, install the Creamerizer Paddle onto the outer bowl lid and lock the lid assembly on the outer bowl. Place the bowl assembly on the motor base and crank the lever to elevate and secure the platform in place. 3. Choose the MILKSHAKE option. 4. Remove the milkshake from the Pint after the processing is finished.
Serving Suggestion: Serve immediately.

Variation Tip: Add nuts of your choice.
Nutritional Information per Serving: Calories 282 | Protein 10g | Carbohydrate 30g | Dietary Fiber 1.5g | Sugar 26g | Fat 14g | Sodium 163mg

Vanilla Cookie Milkshake

Preparation Time: 5 minutes|Servings: 1

Ingredients:

1 ½ cups vanilla ice cream
½ cup oat milk

3 small sugar cookies, crushed
2 tablespoons sprinkles

Preparation:

1. In an empty Ninja Creami pint, place all ingredients and mix well. 2. Arrange the container into the outer bowl of Ninja Creami. 3. Install the "Creamerizer Paddle" onto the lid of the outer bowl. 4. Then rotate the lid clockwise to lock. 5. Turn on the unit. 6. Then select the "MILKSHAKE" function. 7. When the program is completed, turn the outer bowl and release it from the machine. 8. Transfer the shake into serving glasses and serve immediately.

Serving Suggestions: Garnish with sprinkles.
Variation Tip: You can use soy milk.
Nutritional Information per Serving: Calories: 215 | Fat: 10g| Sat Fat: 7g| Carbohydrates: 24g| Fiber: 0.8g| Sugar: 22g| Protein: 2g

Lemon Cookie Milkshake

Preparation Time: 3 Minutes|Cook Time: 5 Minutes|Serves: 4

Ingredients:

1 cup vanilla ice cream
3 lemon cream sandwich cookies

¼ cup milk

Preparation:

1. Add the ice cream, lemon cream cookies, and milk into an empty CREAMi Pint. 2. Place the Pint in the outer bowl, install the Creamerizer Paddle onto the outer bowl lid and lock the lid assembly on the outer bowl. Place the bowl assembly on the motor base and crank the lever to elevate and secure the platform in place. 3. Select the MILKSHAKE option. 4. Remove the milkshake from the Pint after the processing is finished.

Serving Suggestion: Serve with the sprinkling of cinnamon.
Variation Tip: Add nuts of your choice.
Nutritional Information per Serving: Calories 220 | Protein 10g | Carbohydrate 23g | Dietary Fiber 5g | Sugar 17g | Fat 5g | Sodium 200mg

Almond Candy Bar Milkshake

Preparation Time: 2 minutes|Servings: 2

Ingredients:

1½ cups coconut dulce de leche ice cream
½ cup almond milk
2 tablespoons almonds, toasted
and chopped
2 tablespoons vegan chocolate chips
2 tablespoons shredded coconut

Preparation:

1. Place all the ingredients in an empty Ninja CREAMi Pint and mix well. 2. Place the pint into the outer bowl of the Ninja CREAMi. 3. Install the Creamerizer Paddle onto the lid of the outer bowl, then rotate the lid clockwise to lock. 4. Turn on the unit. 5. Press the MILKSHAKE button. 6. When the program is complete, turn the outer bowl and release it from the machine. 7. Transfer the shake into serving glasses and serve immediately.

Serving Suggestions: Garnish with more crushed almonds.
Variation Tip: You can use any milk you prefer.
Nutritional Information per Serving: Calories: 313 | Fat: 23g | Sat Fat: 16g | Carbohydrates: 19g | Fiber: 3g | Sugar: 14g | Protein: 4g

Caramel Milkshake

Preparation Time: 10 minutes|Servings: 2

Ingredients:

¾ cup milk
1½ cups vanilla ice cream
2 tablespoons caramel sauce

Preparation:

1. Put the ice cream, followed by the milk and caramel sauce, in the Ninja CREAMi Pint. 2. Assemble the unit as per the user instructions. 3. Select the MILKSHAKE program. 4. When the program is complete, remove the outer bowl. 5. Transfer the shake into serving glasses and serve immediately.

Serving Suggestions: Serve with a topping of whipped cream and caramel sauce.
Variation Tip: You can also use almond milk.
Nutritional Information per Serving: Calories: 200 | Fat: 7.1g | Sat

Fat: 4.5g | Carbohydrates: 30g |Fiber: 0.6g | Sugar: 14.6g | Protein: 5g

Lime Sherbet Milkshake

Preparation Time: 10 minutes|Servings: 1

Ingredients:

½ cup lime seltzer
1½ cups rainbow sherbet

Preparation:

1. Put the sherbet in the Ninja CREAMi Pint and top it with the lime seltzer. 2. Assemble the unit as per the user instructions. 3. Select the MILKSHAKE program. 4. When the program is complete, remove the outer bowl. 5. Transfer the shake into a serving glass and serve immediately.

Serving Suggestions: Garnish with lime slices and serve cold.
Variation Tip: You can also squeeze in some fresh lime.
Nutritional Information per Serving: Calories: 195 | Fat: 2.3g | Sat Fat: 1.2g | Carbohydrates: 40.5g |Fiber: 0g | Sugar: 30g | Protein: 1.5g

Hazelnut Milkshake

Preparation Time: 5 minutes|Servings: 2

Ingredients:

1 ½ cups hazelnut ice cream
½ cup whole milk
¼ cup chocolate spread

Preparation:

1. In an empty Ninja Creami pint container, place all ingredients and mix together well. 2. Arrange the container into the outer bowl of Ninja Creami. 3. Install the "Creamerizer Paddle" onto the lid of the outer bowl. 4. Then rotate the lid clockwise to lock. 5. Turn on the unit. 6. Then select the "MILKSHAKE" function. 7. When the program is completed, turn the outer bowl and release it from the machine. 8. Transfer the shake into serving glasses and serve immediately.

Serving Suggestions: Serve with the sprinkling of cocoa powder.
Variation Tip: You can use milk of your choice.
Nutritional Information per Serving: Calories: 209 | Fat: 11g| Sat Fat: 5g| Carbohydrates: 21g| Fiber: 0.8g| Sugar: 20g| Protein: 4g

Chocolate Proyo Milkshake

Preparation Time: 2 minutes | Servings: 2

Ingredients:

1 cup chocolate frozen yogurt
1 scoop chocolate protein whey
powder
1 cup whole milk

Preparation:

1. Place all the ingredients in an empty Ninja CREAMi Pint and mix well.
2. Place the pint into the outer bowl of the Ninja CREAMi. 3. Install the Creamerizer Paddle onto the lid of the outer bowl, then rotate the lid clockwise to lock. 4. Turn the unit on. 5. Press the MILKSHAKE button. 6. When the program is complete, turn the outer bowl and release it from the machine. 7. Transfer the shake into serving glasses and serve immediately.

Serving Suggestions: Top with chocolate syrup.
Variation Tip: You can use any milk you prefer.
Nutritional Information per Serving: Calories: 243 | Fat: 7.6g | Sat Fat: 4.3g | Carbohydrates: 28g | Fiber: 0g | Sugar: 25g | Protein: 15g

Lemon Pie Milkshake

Preparation Time: 5 minutes | Servings: 2

Ingredients:

1 ½ cups vanilla ice cream
4 tablespoons lemon curd
½ cup graham crackers, broken

Preparation:

1. In an empty Ninja Creami pint, place all ingredients and mix well. 2. Arrange the container into the outer bowl of Ninja Creami. 3. Install the "Creamerizer Paddle" onto the lid of the outer bowl. 4. Then rotate the lid clockwise to lock. 5. Turn on the unit. 6. Then select the "MILKSHAKE" function. 7. When the program is completed, turn the outer bowl and release it from the machine. 8. Transfer the shake into serving glasses and serve immediately.

Serving Suggestions: Garnish with marshmallows.
Variation Tip: You can use any ice cream.
Nutritional Information per Serving: Calories: 313 | Fat: 17g | Sat Fat: 4g | Carbohydrates: 33g | Fiber: 1g | Sugar: 24g | Protein: 5g

Coconut Cookie Milkshake

Preparation Time: 5 minutes | Servings: 1

Ingredients:

1 cup coconut milk
½ cup amaretto-flavored coffee creamer
1 tablespoon agave nectar
¼ cup chopped chocolate chip cookies

Preparation:

1. Place all ingredients except the chocolate chip cookies in an empty Ninja Creami pint and mix well. 2. Close the pint with a pint lid and place into a freezer. Freeze for 24 hours. 3. Arrange the uncovered container into the outer bowl of Ninja Creami. 4. Install the "Creamerizer Paddle" onto the lid of the outer bowl. 5. Then rotate the lid clockwise to lock. 6. Turn on the unit. 7. Then select the "MILKSHAKE" function. 8. When the program is completed, remove the lid. Create a 1 ½-inch wide hole at the center that reaches the bottom of the pint with a spoon. 9. Add the chocolate chip cookies to the hole, replace the lid, and use 'MIX-IN' function. 10. Transfer the shake into serving glasses and serve immediately.

Serving Suggestions: Serve with the sprinkling of cocoa powder.
Variation Tip: You can use milk of your choice.
Nutritional Information per Serving: Calories: 542 | Fat: 16g | Sat Fat: 8g | Carbohydrates: 34g | Fiber: 0.1g | Sugar: 54g | Protein: 8g

Tahini Oat Milkshake

Preparation Time: 5 minutes | Servings: 1

Ingredients:

1 ½ cups chocolate ice cream
½ cup oat milk
¼ cup tahini
2 tablespoons coffee

Preparation:

1. In an empty Ninja Creami pint, place all ingredients and mix well. 2. Arrange the container into the outer bowl of Ninja Creami. 3. Install the "Creamerizer Paddle" onto the lid of the outer bowl. 4. Then rotate the lid clockwise to lock. 5. Turn on the unit. 6. Then select the "MILKSHAKE" function. 7. When the program is completed, turn the outer bowl and release it from the machine. 8. Transfer the shake into serving glasses and serve immediately.

Serving Suggestions: Garnish with coffee powder.
Variation Tip: You can use any milk.
Nutritional Information per Serving: Calories: 432 | Fat: 34g | Sat Fat: 7g | Carbohydrates: 45g | Fiber: 11g | Sugar: 15g | Protein: 15g

Mocha Milkshake

Preparation Time: 10 minutes|Servings: 2

Ingredients:

1½ cups chocolate ice cream
½ cup cashew milk
½ cup ripe banana, peeled and cut

into ½-inch pieces
1 tablespoon instant coffee powder

Preparation:

1. In an empty Ninja CREAMi pint container, place ice cream followed by milk, banana and coffee powder. 2. Arrange the container into the Outer Bowl of Ninja CREAMi. 3. Install the Creamerizer Paddle onto the lid of Outer Bowl. 4. Then rotate the lid clockwise to lock. 5. Press Power button to turn on the unit. 6. Then press Milkshake button. 7. When the program is completed, turn the Outer Bowl and release it from the machine. 8. Transfer the shake into serving glasses and serve immediately.

Serving Suggestions: Serve with the topping of chocolate shaving.
Variation Tip: Make sure to use ripe banana.
Nutritional Information per Serving: Calories: 142 | Fat: 5.9g|Sat Fat: 3.4g|Carbohydrates: 20.8g|Fiber: 1.4g|Sugar: 15.1g|Protein: 2.2g

Mint Cookie Milkshake

Preparation Time: 5 minutes|Servings: 4

Ingredients:

1 ½ cups mint ice cream
3 cream cookies

¼ cup milk

Preparation:

1. In an empty Ninja Creami pint, place all ingredients and mix well. 2. Arrange the container into the outer bowl of Ninja Creami. 3. Install the "Creamerizer Paddle" onto the lid of the outer bowl. 4. Then rotate the lid clockwise to lock. 5. Turn on the unit. 6. Then select the "MILKSHAKE" function. 7. When the program is completed, turn the outer bowl and release it from the machine. 8. Transfer the shake into serving glasses and serve immediately.

Serving Suggestions: Top with whipped cream.
Variation Tip: You can use any ice cream.

Nutritional Information per Serving: Calories: 113 | Fat: 2g| Sat Fat: 0.8g| Carbohydrates: 21g| Fiber: 0.6g| Sugar: 6.7g| Protein: 3g

Coconut Lemon Milkshake

Preparation Time: 5 minutes|Servings: 2

Ingredients:

½ can coconut milk, about 7 ounces
¼ cup sugar, granulated

½ teaspoon vanilla extract
½ teaspoon lemon extract

Preparation:

1. Whisk the coconut milk until smooth in a medium mixing bowl. Then mix in the remaining ingredients. 2. Pour mixture in an empty Ninja Creami pint. 3. Arrange the container into the outer bowl of Ninja Creami. 4. Install the "Creamerizer Paddle" onto the lid of the outer bowl. 5. Then rotate the lid clockwise to lock. 6. Turn on the unit. 7. Then select the "MILKSHAKE" function. 8. When the program is completed, turn the outer bowl and release it from the machine. 9. Transfer the shake into serving glasses and serve immediately.

Serving Suggestions: Top with whipped cream.
Variation Tip: You can use any milk.
Nutritional Information per Serving: Calories: 118 | Fat: 0.1g| Sat Fat: 0g| Carbohydrates: 28g| Fiber: 3g| Sugar: 25g| Protein: 2g

Chocolate Liqueur Milkshake

Preparation Time: 10 minutes|Servings: 2

Ingredients:

⅓ cup chocolate liqueur
2 cups vanilla ice cream

⅓ cup whole milk

Preparation:

1. Put the ice cream, followed by the chocolate liqueur and milk, in the Ninja CREAMi Pint. 2. Assemble the unit as per the user instructions. 3. Select the MILKSHAKE program. 4. When the program is complete, remove the outer bowl. 5. Transfer the shake into serving glasses and serve immediately.

Serving Suggestions: Serve garnished with whipped cream and ground cinnamon.
Variation Tip: You can use chocolate ice cream instead of vanilla.
Nutritional Information per Serving: Calories: 324 | Fat: 8.5g | Sat Fat: 4g | Carbohydrates: 34.9g |Fiber: 0.5g | Sugar: 33.2g | Protein: 3.7g

Peanut Butter Brownie Milkshake

Preparation Time: 5 Minutes|Cook Time: 5 Minutes|Serves: 2

Ingredients:

½ cup chocolate ice cream
½ cup whole milk
2 tablespoons peanut butter, for

mix-in
1¼ cups brownies, chopped into
bite-sized pieces, for mix-in

Preparation:

1. Place the ice cream in an empty CREAMi Pint. 2. Use a spoon to create a 1½-inch wide hole that reaches the bottom of the Pint. Add the remaining ingredients to the hole. 3. Place Pint in outer bowl, install Creamerizer Paddle onto outer bowl lid and lock the lid assembly on the outer bowl. Place the bowl assembly on the motor base and crank the lever to elevate and secure the platform in place. 4. Select MILKSHAKE. 5. Remove the milkshake from the Pint after the processing is finished.

Serving Suggestion: Serve immediately.
Variation Tip: Add nuts of your choice.
Nutritional Information per Serving: Calories 596 | Protein 5g | Carbohydrate 38g | Dietary Fiber 0.5g | Sugar 22g | Fat 1g | Sodium 106mg

Baileys Milkshake

Preparation Time: 5 Minutes|Cook Time: 5 Minutes|Serves: 1

Ingredients:

1 scoop vanilla ice cream
1 scoop chocolate ice cream
1 tablespoon chocolate sauce

1 tablespoon caramel sauce
2 fluid ounces Baileys Irish Cream
1 cup whole milk

Preparation:

1. Place all ingredients into an empty CREAMi Pint. 2. Place Pint in outer bowl, install Creamerizer Paddle onto outer bowl lid and lock the lid assembly on the outer bowl. Place the bowl assembly on the motor base and crank the lever to elevate and secure the platform in place. 3. Choose the MILKSHAKE option. 4. Remove the milkshake from the Pint after the processing is finished.

Serving Suggestion: Serve with a topping of whipping cream.
Variation Tip: Add nuts of your choice.
Nutritional Information per Serving: Calories 718 | Protein 18g | Carbohydrate 85g | Dietary Fiber 1.1g | Sugar 63g | Fat 22g | Sodium 369mg

Almond Butter Milkshake

Preparation Time: 5 minutes|Servings: 2

Ingredients:

1 cup vanilla ice cream
¼ cup whole milk

1 tablespoon almond butter

Preparation:

1. In an empty Ninja Creami pint, place all ingredients and mix well. 2. Arrange the container into the outer bowl of Ninja Creami. 3. Install the "Creamerizer Paddle" onto the lid of the outer bowl. 4. Then rotate the lid clockwise to lock. 5. Turn on the unit. 6. Then select the "MILKSHAKE" function. 7. When the program is completed, turn the outer bowl and release it from the machine. 8. Transfer the shake into serving glasses and serve immediately.

Serving Suggestions: Top with whipped cream.
Variation Tip: You can use coconut milk.
Nutritional Information per Serving: Calories: 384 | Fat: 10.6g| Sat Fat: 2g| Carbohydrates: 70g| Fiber: 0.8g| Sugar: 32g| Protein: 10g

Ginger Cranberry Milkshake

Preparation Time: 5 minutes|Servings: 2

Ingredients:

1 ½ cups cranberry ice cream   1 teaspoon ground ginger
½ cup oat milk

Preparation:

1. In an empty Ninja Creami pint, place all ingredients and mix well. 2. Arrange the container into the outer bowl of Ninja Creami. 3. Install the "Creamerizer Paddle" onto the lid of the outer bowl. 4. Then rotate the lid clockwise to lock. 5. Turn on the unit. 6. Then select the "MILKSHAKE" function. 7. When the program is completed, turn the outer bowl and release it from the machine. 8. Transfer the shake into serving glasses and serve immediately.

Serving Suggestions: Top with grated chocolate.
Variation Tip: You can use coconut milk.
Nutritional Information per Serving: Calories: 318 | Fat: 16g| Sat Fat: 10g| Carbohydrates: 34g| Fiber: 2g| Sugar: 31g| Protein: 2g

Banana Milkshake

Preparation Time: 5 Minutes|Cook Time: 5 Minutes|Serves: 1

Ingredients:

1 cup whole milk   2 tablespoons sugar
1 medium-size banana

Preparation:

1. Place all ingredients into an empty CREAMi Pint. 2. Place Pint in outer bowl, install Creamerizer Paddle onto outer bowl lid and lock the lid assembly on the outer bowl. Place the bowl assembly on the motor base and crank the lever to elevate and secure the platform in place. 3. Choose MILKSHAKE. 4. Remove the milkshake from the Pint after the processing is finished.

Serving Suggestion: Serve cold.
Variation Tip: Add some chocolate and nuts if you prefer.
Nutritional Information per Serving: Calories 166 | Protein 5.3g | Carbohydrate 30.1g | Dietary Fiber 3g | Sugar 20g | Fat 2.8g | Sodium 51.2mg

Healthy Strawberry Shake

Preparation Time: 10 Minutes|Cook Time: 10 Minutes|Serves: 1

Ingredients:

1 cup milk   ½ teaspoon vanilla extract
1 tablespoon honey   ½ cup frozen strawberries

Preparation:

1. Add the milk, honey, vanilla extract, and strawberries into an empty CREAMi Pint. 2. Place Pint in outer bowl, install Creamerizer Paddle onto outer bowl lid and lock the lid assembly on the outer bowl. Place the bowl assembly on the motor base and crank the lever to elevate and secure the platform in place. 3. Select MILKSHAKE. 4. Remove the milkshake from the Pint after the processing is finished.

Serving Suggestion: Serve cold.
Variation Tip: You can top the shake with a drizzle of chocolate syrup.
Nutritional Information per Serving: Calories 186 | Protein 8.4g | Carbohydrate 27g | Dietary Fiber 1.5g | Sugar 23g | Fat 5g | Sodium 102mg

Walnut Milkshake

Preparation Time: 10 minutes|Servings: 2

Ingredients:

1½ cups vanilla ice cream
½ cup coconut milk
2 tablespoons maple syrup

¼ cup walnuts, chopped
Pinch of salt

Preparation:
1. Put the ice cream, followed by the soy milk, maple syrup, pecans, cinnamon, and salt, in the Ninja CREAMi Pint. 2. Assemble the unit as per the user instructions. 3. Select the MILKSHAKE program. 4. When the program is complete, remove the outer bowl. 5. Transfer the shake into serving glasses and serve immediately.

Serving Suggestions: Serve with a topping of crushed walnuts and ground cinnamon.
Variation Tip: You can also make this milkshake with pecans.
Nutritional Information per Serving: Calories: 390 | Fat: 28.8g | Sat Fat: 16.6g | Carbohydrates: 30.3g | Fiber: 2.8g | Sugar: 24.6g | Protein: 6.9g

Sugar Cookie Milkshake

Preparation Time: 10 minutes|Servings: 1

Ingredients:

½ cup oat milk
½ cup vanilla ice cream

3 small sugar cookies, crushed
2 tablespoons sprinkles

Preparation:
1. Put the vanilla ice cream in the Ninja CREAMi Pint. 2. With a spoon, create a 1½-inch wide hole in the center of the ice cream that reaches the bottom of the pint. 3. Put the oat milk, sugar cookies, and sprinkles into the hole. 4. Assemble the unit as per the user instructions. 5. Press the MILKSHAKE program. 6. When the program is complete, remove the outer bowl. 7. Transfer the shake into a serving glass and serve immediately.

Serving Suggestions: Serve with a topping of mini marshmallows.
Variation Tip: Feel free to use any milk of your choice.
Nutritional Information per Serving: Calories: 283 | Fat: 5.1g | Sat Fat: 2.1g | Carbohydrates: 57.8g |Fiber: 5.1g | Sugar: 32.5g | Protein: 5.6g

Coffee Vodka Milkshake

Preparation Time: 10 minutes|Servings: 2

Ingredients:

2 tablespoons coffee liqueur
2 cups vanilla ice cream

2 tablespoons vodka

Preparation:
1. Put the ice cream, followed by the coffee liqueur and vodka, in the Ninja CREAMi Pint. 2. Assemble the unit as per the user instructions. 3. Select the MILKSHAKE program. 4. When the program is complete, remove the outer bowl. 5. Transfer the shake into serving glasses and serve immediately.

Serving Suggestions: Serve with whipped cream and cherries.
Variation Tip: You can also add coffee-flavored ice cream.
Nutritional Information per Serving: Calories: 226 | Fat: 7.1g | Sat Fat: 3.2g | Carbohydrates: 24.1g |Fiber: 0.5g | Sugar: 22.1g | Protein: 2.3g

Pecan Milkshake

Preparation Time: 5 minutes|Servings: 1

Ingredients:
1 ½ cups vanilla ice cream
½ cup unsweetened oat
¼ cup chopped pecans
1 teaspoon ground cinnamon

Preparation:
1. In an empty Ninja Creami pint, place all ingredients and mix well. 2. Arrange the container into the outer bowl of Ninja Creami. 3. Install the "Creamerizer Paddle" onto the lid of the outer bowl. 4. Then rotate the lid clockwise to lock. 5. Turn on the unit. 6. Then select the "MILKSHAKE" function. 7. When the program is completed, turn the outer bowl and release it from the machine. 8. Transfer the shake into serving glasses and serve immediately.

Serving Suggestions: Garnish with coffee powder.
Variation Tip: You can use soy milk.
Nutritional Information per Serving: Calories: 694 | Fat: 28g| Sat Fat: 3g| Carbohydrates: 99g| Fiber: 12g| Sugar: 20g| Protein: 20g

Cashew Banana Milkshake

Preparation Time: 5 minutes|Servings: 2

Ingredients:
1 ½ cups chocolate ice cream
½ cup cashew milk
½ cup ripe banana, cut into pieces
1 tablespoon instant coffee powder

Preparation:
1. In an empty Ninja Creami pint, place all ingredients and mix well. 2. Arrange the container into the outer bowl of Ninja Creami. 3. Install the "Creamerizer Paddle" onto the lid of the outer bowl. 4. Then rotate the lid clockwise to lock. 5. Turn on the unit. 6. Then select the "MILKSHAKE" function. 7. When the program is completed, turn the outer bowl and release it from the machine. 8. Transfer the shake into serving glasses and serve immediately.

Serving Suggestions: Garnish with coffee powder.
Variation Tip: You can use any milk.
Nutritional Information per Serving: Calories: 269 | Fat: 12g| Sat Fat: 7.7g| Carbohydrates: 40g| Fiber: 2.4g| Sugar: 32g| Protein: 4g

Strawberry Banana Smoothie Bowl

Preparation Time: 10 minutes|Servings: 4

Ingredients:

1 cup fresh ripe banana, sliced
1 cup ripe strawberries, trimmed and sliced
2 tablespoons vanilla protein powder
¼ cup raw agave nectar
¼ cup whole milk
¼ cup pineapple juice

Preparation:
1. Fill an empty CREAMi Pint to the MAX FILL line with the bananas and strawberries and mix evenly. 2. Mix all the ingredients until well combined in a large bowl. 3. Transfer the mixture into an empty Ninja CREAMi Pint. 4. Cover the pint with the lid and freeze for 24 hours. 5. After 24 hours, remove the lid from the container and place the pint into the outer bowl of the Ninja CREAMi. 6. Install the Creamerizer Paddle onto the lid of the outer bowl, then rotate the lid clockwise to lock. 7. Turn the unit on. 8. Press the SMOOTHIE BOWL button. 9. When the program is complete, turn the outer bowl and release it from the machine. 10. Transfer the smoothie into serving bowls and serve with your favorite toppings.

Serving Suggestions: Top with any fresh fruit.
Variation Tip: You can also use almond milk.
Nutritional Information per Serving: Calories: 115 | Fat: 0.7g | Sat Fat: 0.3g | Carbohydrates: 24g | Fiber: 1g | Sugar: 23g | Protein: 1g

Fruity Coffee Smoothie Bowl

Preparation Time: 10 minutes|Servings: 4

Ingredients:

1 cup brewed coffee
2 tablespoons almond butter
1 large banana, peeled and sliced
½ cup oat milk
1 cup fresh raspberries

Preparation:
1. Throw all the ingredients in a high-powered blender and pulse until smooth. 2. Transfer the mixture into the Ninja CREAMi Pint. 3. Snap the lid on the pint and freeze it for 24 hours. 4. Remove the lid and assemble the unit as per the user instructions. 5. Select the SMOOTHIE BOWL program. 6. When the program is complete, remove the outer bowl. 7. Transfer the smoothie into serving bowls and serve immediately.

Serving Suggestions: Top with granola.
Variation Tip: You can also use other berries.
Nutritional Information per Serving: Calories: 108 | Fat: 5.1g | Sat Fat: 1.4g | Carbohydrates: 14.9g | Fiber: 3.8g | Sugar: 7.7g | Protein: 3g

Kale, Avocado & fruit Smoothie Bowl

Preparation Time: 10 minutes|Servings: 4

Ingredients:

1 banana, peeled and cut into 1-inch pieces
½ of avocado, peeled, pitted and cut into 1-inch pieces
1 cup fresh kale leaves
1 cup green apple, peeled, cored and cut into 1-inch pieces
¼ cup unsweetened coconut milk
2 tablespoons agave nectar

Preparation:
1. In a large high-speed blender, add all the ingredients and pulse until smooth. 2. Transfer the mixture into an empty Ninja CREAMi pint container. 3. Cover the container with storage lid and freeze for 24 hours. 4. After 24 hours, remove the lid from container and arrange into the Outer Bowl of Ninja CREAMi. 5. Install the Creamerizer Paddle onto the lid of Outer Bowl. 6. Then rotate the lid clockwise to lock. 7. Press Power button to turn on the unit. 8. Then press Smoothie Bowl button. 9. When the program is completed, turn the Outer Bowl and release it from the machine. 10. Transfer the smoothie into serving bowls and serve immediately.

Serving Suggestions: Serve with the topping of fresh berries and coconut.
Variation Tip: Kale can be replaced with spinach.
Nutritional Information per Serving: Calories: 179 | Fat: 8.7g|Sat Fat: 4.2g|Carbohydrates: 27.2g|Fiber: 4.9g|Sugar: 17.5g|Protein: 1.8g

Frozen Fruit Smoothie Bowl

Preparation Time: 10 minutes | Servings: 2

Ingredients:

2 cups frozen fruit mix
1 ripe banana, peeled and cut into

1-inch pieces
1¼ cups vanilla yogurt

Preparation:

1. Add all the ingredients to a high-speed blender and pulse until smooth. 2. Transfer the mixture to the Ninja CREAMi Pint. 3. Snap the lid on the pint and freeze it for 24 hours. 4. Remove the lid and assemble the unit as per the user instructions. 5. Select the SMOOTHIE BOWL program. 6. When the program is complete, remove the outer bowl. 7. Transfer the smoothie into serving bowls and serve immediately.

Serving Suggestions: Top with banana slices, blueberries, and chopped almonds.
Variation Tip: You can use Greek yogurt.
Nutritional Information per Serving: Calories: 251 | Fat: 2.1g | Sat Fat: 1.4g | Carbohydrates: 45.2g |Fiber: 4.5g | Sugar: 29.9g | Protein: 10.8g

Strawberry-Orange Creme Smoothie

Preparation Time: 5 Minutes | Cook Time: 5 Minutes | Serves: 1

Ingredients:

1 (5.3 ounces) container Yoplait Greek 100 orange creme yogurt
½ cup fresh strawberries, hulled

¼ cup ice cubes (optional)
¼ cup orange juice

Preparation:

1. Put all the ingredients into an empty ninja CREAMi Pint. 2. Place the Ninja CREAMi Pint into the outer bowl. Place the outer bowl with the Pint in it into the ninja CREAMi machine and turn until the outer bowl locks into place. Push the SMOOTHIE button. During the SMOOTHIE function, the ingredients will mix together and become very creamy. 3. Once the SMOOTHIE function has ended, turn the outer bowl and release it from the ninja CREAMi machine. 4. Scoop the smoothie into a tall glass.

Serving suggestion: Serve immediately.
Variation Tip: Add some fresh mint on top.
Nutritional Information per Serving: Calories 136 | Protein 12g | Carbohydrate 20g | Dietary Fiber 1.5g | Sugar 6g | Fat 0.3g | Sodium 103mg

Chocolate, Peanut Butter & Banana Smoothie

Preparation Time: 5 Minutes | Cook Time: 5 Minutes | Serves: 2

Ingredients:

1 (3¼ ounces) cup chocolate pudding
1 tablespoon creamy peanut butter
1 large ripe banana, cut into pieces

⅔ cup reduced-fat (2%) milk
½ cup ice cubes
Reddi-wip chocolate dairy whipped topping

Preparation:

1. Mash the bananas in a large bowl and add all the other ingredients except for the whipped topping. Combine and put into the ninja CREAMi Pint. 2. Place the Pint into the outer bowl. Place the outer bowl with the Pint in it into the ninja CREAMi machine and turn until the outer bowl locks into place. Push the SMOOTHIE button. The ingredients will mix together and become very creamy. 3. Once the SMOOTHIE function has ended, turn the outer bowl and release it from the ninja CREAMi machine. 4. Scoop the smoothie into glass bowls to serve.

Serving Suggestion: Serve topped with banana slices, chocolate shavings, and whipped cream.
Variation Tip: Add chopped nuts of your choice.
Nutritional Information per Serving: Calories 221 | Protein 4g | Carbohydrate 30g | Dietary Fiber 3.5g | Sugar 11g | Fat 7.6g | Sodium 113mg

Mango Smoothie Bowl

Preparation Time: 10 minutes|Servings: 4

Ingredients:

2 cups ripe mango, peeled, pitted and cut into 1-inch pieces

1 (14-ounces) can of unsweetened coconut milk

Preparation:

1. Place the mango pieces into an empty Ninja CREAMi pint container. 2. Top with coconut milk and stir to combine. 3. Cover the container with storage lid and freeze for 24 hours. 4. After 24 hours, remove the lid from container and arrange into the Outer Bowl of Ninja CREAMi. 5. Install the Creamerizer Paddle onto the lid of Outer Bowl. 6. Then rotate the lid clockwise to lock. 7. Press Power button to turn on the unit. 8. Then press Smoothie Bowl button. 9. When the program is completed, turn the Outer Bowl and release it from the machine. 10. Transfer the smoothie into serving bowls and serve immediately.

Serving Suggestions: Serve with the topping of fresh fruit and coconut.
Variation Tip: You can drizzle this smoothie bowl with some honey.
Nutritional Information per Serving: Calories: 198 | Fat: 14g|Sat Fat: 12.5g|Carbohydrates: 14.8g|Fiber: 1.3g|Sugar: 13.8g|Protein: 1.g

Dragon Fruit & Pineapple Smoothie Bowl

Preparation Time: 10 minutes|Servings: 4

Ingredients:

2 cups frozen dragon fruit chunks

2 (6-ounces) cans pineapple juice

Preparation:

1. Place the dragon fruit chunks into an empty Ninja CREAMi pint container. 2. Top with pineapple juice and stir to combine. 3. Cover the container with storage lid and freeze for 24 hours. 4. After 24 hours, remove the lid from container and arrange into the Outer Bowl of Ninja CREAMi. 5. Install the Creamerizer Paddle onto the lid of Outer Bowl. 6. Then rotate the lid clockwise to lock. 7. Press Power button to turn on the unit. 8. Then press Smoothie Bowl button. 9. When the program is completed, turn the Outer Bowl and release it from the machine. 10. Transfer the smoothie into serving bowls and serve immediately.

Serving Suggestions: Serve with the topping of fruit, chia seeds and granola.
Variation Tip: If you like sweeter smoothie, then use some sweetener.
Nutritional Information per Serving: Calories: 68 | Fat: 0.1g|Sat Fat: 0g|Carbohydrates: 17g|Fiber: 0.2g|Sugar: 14.5g|Protein: 0.3g

Green Monster Smoothie

Preparation Time: 10 Minutes|Cook Time: 10 Minutes|Serves: 1

Ingredients:

½ cup baby spinach
½ apple, peeled, cored, and chopped
½ banana, sliced

¼ cup chopped carrots
¼ cup orange juice
¼ cup fresh strawberries
¼ cup ice

Preparation:

1. Put the spinach, apples, bananas, carrots, orange juice, strawberries, and ice into an empty ninja CREAMi Pint. 2. Place the Ninja CREAMi Pint into the outer bowl. Place the outer bowl with the Pint in it into the ninja CREAMi machine and turn until the outer bowl locks into place. Push the SMOOTHIE button. During the SMOOTHIE function, the ingredients will mix together and become very creamy. 3. Once the SMOOTHIE function has ended, turn the outer bowl and release it from the ninja CREAMi machine. 4. Scoop the smoothie into a glass.

Serving Suggestion: Serve immediately.
Variation Tip: Add some fresh mint or basil.
Nutritional Information per Serving: Calories 146 | Protein 2.2g | Carbohydrate 36g | Dietary Fiber 5.3g | Sugar 23g | Fat 0.7g | Sodium 38mg

Oat Banana Smoothie Bowl

Preparation Time: 10 minutes|Cooking Time: 1 minute|Servings: 2

Ingredients:

½ cup water
¼ cup quick oats
1 cup vanilla Greek yogurt
½ cup banana, peeled and sliced
3 tablespoons honey

Preparation:

1. In a small microwave-safe bowl, add the water and oats and microwave on High or about one minute. 2. Remove from the microwave and stir in the yogurt, banana and honey until well combined. 3. Transfer the mixture into an empty Ninja CREAMi pint container. 4. Cover the container with storage lid and freeze for 24 hours. 5. After 24 hours, remove the lid from container and arrange into the Outer Bowl of Ninja CREAMi. 6. Install the Creamerizer Paddle onto the lid of Outer Bowl. 7. Then rotate the lid clockwise to lock. 8. Press Power button to turn on the unit. 9. Then press Smoothie Bowl button. 10. When the program is completed, turn the Outer Bowl and release it from the machine. 11. Transfer the smoothie into serving bowls and serve with your favorite topping.

Serving Suggestions: Serve with the topping of banana, granola and nuts.
Variation Tip: You can use plain yogurt too.
Nutritional Information per Serving: Calories: 278 | Fat: 2.7g|Sat Fat: 1.1g|Carbohydrates: 55.7g|Fiber: 2.1g|Sugar: 41.6g|Protein: 10.9g

Strawberry Smoothie Bowl

Preparation Time: 10 minutes|Servings: 4

Ingredients:

2 tablespoons vanilla protein powder
¼ cup agave nectar
¼ cup pineapple juice
½ cup whole milk
1 cup ripe banana, peeled and cut in ½-inch pieces
1 cup fresh strawberries, hulled and quartered

Preparation:

1. In a large bowl, add the protein powder, agave nectar, pineapple juice and milk and beat until well combined. 2. Place the banana and strawberry into an empty Ninja CREAMi pint container and with the back of a spoon, firmly press the fruit below the Max Fill line. 3. Top with milk mixture and mix until well combined. 4. Cover the container with storage lid and freeze for 24 hours. 5. After 24 hours, remove the lid from container and arrange into the Outer Bowl of Ninja CREAMi. 6. Install the Creamerizer Paddle onto the lid of Outer Bowl. 7. Then rotate the lid clockwise to lock. 8. Press Power button to turn on the unit. 9. Then press Smoothie Bowl button. 10. When the program is completed, turn the Outer Bowl and release it from the machine. 11. Transfer the smoothie into serving bowls and serve immediately.

Serving Suggestions: Serve with the topping of fresh strawberry slices, coconut and chocolate shaving.
Variation Tip: You can adjust the ratio of sweetener according to your taste.
Nutritional Information per Serving: Calories: 145 | Fat: 1.3g|Sat Fat: 0.6g|Carbohydrates: 31g|Fiber: 2.7g|Sugar: 24.7g|Protein: 4.7g

Vegan Coffee Smoothie Bowl

Preparation Time: 10 minutes|Servings: 3

Ingredients:

¼ cup instant coffee
2 cups vanilla unsweetened
almond milk

Preparation:

1. Whisk the instant coffee and almond milk in a large mixing bowl until thoroughly combined and the coffee has dissolved. 2. Transfer the mixture into an empty Ninja CREAMi Pint. 3. Cover the pint with the lid and freeze for 24 hours. 4. After 24 hours, remove the lid and place the pint into the outer bowl of the Ninja CREAMi. 5. Install the Creamerizer Paddle onto the lid of the outer bowl, then rotate the lid clockwise to lock. 6. Turn the unit on. 7. Press the SMOOTHIE BOWL button. 8. When the program is completed, turn the outer bowl and release it from the machine. 9. Transfer the smoothie into serving bowls and serve with your favorite toppings.

Serving Suggestions: Top with chocolate chunks.
Variation Tip: You can also use vanilla milk.
Nutritional Information per Serving: Calories: 330 | Fat: 34g | Sat Fat: 21g | Carbohydrates: 7g | Fiber: 3g | Sugar: 5g | Protein: 3g

Apricot Smoothie Bowl

Preparation Time: 10 minutes | Servings: 3

Ingredients:

1 (14-ounce) can unsweetened coconut milk

2 cups apricots, pitted and cut into 1-inch pieces

Preparation:

1. Place the mango pieces into the Ninja CREAMi Pint. 2. Top with the coconut milk and stir to combine. 3. Snap the lid on the pint and freeze it for 24 hours. 4. Remove the lid and assemble the unit as per the user instructions. 5. Select the SMOOTHIE BOWL program. 6. When the program is complete, remove the outer bowl. 7. Transfer the smoothie into serving bowls and serve immediately.

Serving Suggestions: Serve with a topping of apricot chunks and granola.

Variation Tip: Add a drizzle of honey.

Nutritional Information per Serving: Calories: 354 | Fat: 32.2g | Sat Fat: 28g | Carbohydrates: 18.7g | Fiber: 4.9g | Sugar: 13.8g | Protein: 4.4g

Raspberry and Orange Smoothie Bowl

Preparation Time: 10 minutes | Servings: 2

Ingredients:

½ cup vanilla yogurt

2 cups fresh raspberries

¼ cup fresh orange juice

1 tablespoon honey

Preparation:

1. Put the raspberries in the Ninja CREAMi Pint. With the back of a spoon, firmly press the berries below the MAX FILL line. 2. Add the

yogurt, orange juice, and honey and stir to combine. 3. Snap the lid on the pint and freeze it for 24 hours. 4. Remove the lid and assemble the unit as per the user instructions. 5. Select the SMOOTHIE BOWL program. 6. When the program is complete, remove the outer bowl. 7. Transfer the smoothie into serving bowls and serve immediately.

Serving Suggestions: Top with sliced almonds, oranges, and raspberries.

Variation Tip: Cashew butter can be used instead of almond butter.

Nutritional Information per Serving: Calories: 153 | Fat: 1.6g | Sat Fat: 0.2g | Carbohydrates: 30.9g | Fiber: 8.1g | Sugar: 21g | Protein: 5.2g

Gator Smoothies

Preparation Time: 5 Minutes | Cook Time: 5 Minutes | Serves: 1

Ingredients:

1 cup ice

1 cup grape-flavored sports drink

1 scoop vanilla ice cream

Preparation:

1. Add the ice, sports drink, and ice cream into an empty ninja CREAMi Pint. 2. Place the Ninja CREAMi Pint into the outer bowl. Place the outer bowl with the Pint in it into the ninja CREAMi machine and turn until the outer bowl locks into place. Push the SMOOTHIE button. During the SMOOTHIE function, the ingredients will mix together and become very creamy. 3. Once the SMOOTHIE function has ended, turn the outer bowl and release it from the ninja CREAMi machine. 4. Pour into a tall glass.

Serving Suggestion: Serve immediately.

Variation Tip: Add nuts of your choice.

Nutritional Information per Serving: Calories 96 | Protein 0.7g | Carbohydrate 18g | Dietary Fiber 0.1g | Sugar 18g | Fat 2.1g | Sodium 53.5mg

Crazy Fruit Smoothie

Preparation Time: 10 Minutes|Cook Time: 10 Minutes|Serves: 1

Ingredients:

1 cup crushed ice
1 banana, chopped
1 kiwi, peeled and chopped
½ cup chopped strawberries
½ cup chopped pineapple
¼ cup cream of coconut
1 tablespoon coconut flakes, for garnish

Preparation:
1. Add the ice, banana, kiwi, strawberries, pineapple, and cream of coconut into an empty ninja CREAMi Pint 2. Place the Ninja CREAMi Pint into the outer bowl. Place the outer bowl with the Pint in it into the ninja CREAMi machine and turn until the outer bowl locks into place. Push the SMOOTHIE button. During the SMOOTHIE function, the ingredients will mix together and become very creamy. 3. Once the SMOOTHIE function has ended, turn the outer bowl and release it from the ninja CREAMi machine. 4. Pour the smoothie into a tall glass.

Serving suggestion: Serve immediately.
Variation Tip: Add berries on top.
Nutritional Information per Serving: Calories 96 | Protein 6g | Carbohydrate 18g | Dietary Fiber 0.5g | Sugar 2g | Fat 0.1g | Sodium 156mg

Avocado and Banana Smoothie Bowl

Preparation Time: 10 minutes|Servings: 4

Ingredients:

½ cup unsweetened coconut milk
¼ cup fresh apple juice
2 tablespoons whey protein isolate
1 cup fresh banana, peeled and cut into ½-inch pieces
1 cup ripe avocado, peeled, pitted, and cut into ½-inch pieces
¼ teaspoon vanilla extract
5 tablespoons maple syrup

Preparation:
1. Put the coconut milk, apple juice, protein isolate, maple syrup, and vanilla extract in a large-sized bowl and beat until well combined. 2. Place the avocado and banana into the Ninja CREAMi Pint. With the back of a spoon, firmly press the fruit below the MAX FILL line. 3. Top with the coconut milk mixture and mix until well combined. 4. Snap the lid on the pint and freeze it for 24 hours. 5. Remove the lid and assemble the unit as per the user instructions. 6. Select the SMOOTHIE BOWL program. 7. When the program is complete, remove the outer bowl. 8. Transfer the smoothie into serving bowls and serve immediately.

Serving Suggestions: Top with bananas, almonds, and flaxseeds.
Variation Tip: You can also use vanilla milk.
Nutritional Information per Serving: Calories: 179 | Fat: 8.7g | Sat Fat: 4.4g | Carbohydrates: 27.2g |Fiber: 4.9g | Sugar: 17.5g | Protein: 1.8g

Mango & Raspberry Smoothie Bowl

Preparation Time: 10 minutes|Servings: 2

Ingredients:

¾ cup frozen mango chunks
½ cup frozen raspberries
½ cup whole milk Greek yogurt
2 tablespoons avocado flesh
1 tablespoon agave nectar

Preparation:
1. In a large bowl, add all the ingredients and mix well. 2. Transfer the mixture into an empty Ninja CREAMi pint container. 3. Cover the container with storage lid and freeze for 24 hours. 4. After 24 hours, remove the lid from container and arrange into the Outer Bowl of Ninja CREAMi. 5. Install the Creamerizer Paddle onto the lid of Outer Bowl. 6. Then rotate the lid clockwise to lock. 7. Press Power button to turn on the unit. 8. Then press Smoothie Bowl button. 9. When the program is completed, turn the Outer Bowl and release it from the machine. 10. Transfer the smoothie into serving bowls and serve immediately.

Serving Suggestions: Serve with the topping of mango, raspberries and coconut.
Variation Tip: Use flesh of ripe avocado.
Nutritional Information per Serving: Calories: 163 | Fat: 5g|Sat Fat: 3.5g|Carbohydrates: 27.4g|Fiber: 3.5g|Sugar: 23.4g|Protein: 3.9g

Honey Berry Smoothie Bowl

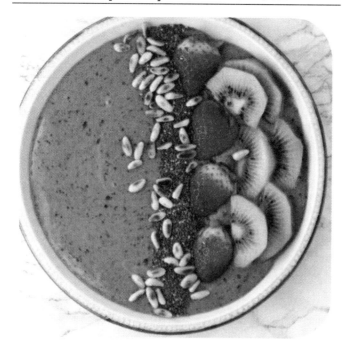

Preparation Time: 10 minutes|Servings: 4

Ingredients:

1 cup fresh blueberries
1 cup fresh blackberries
1 cup fresh raspberries
¼ cup yogurt
1 tablespoon honey

Preparation:
1. Mix all the ingredients until well combined in a large bowl. 2. Transfer the mixture into an empty Ninja CREAMi Pint. 3. Cover the pint with the lid and freeze for 24 hours. 4. After 24 hours, remove the lid and place the pint into the outer bowl of the Ninja CREAMi. 5. Install the Creamerizer Paddle onto the lid of the outer bowl, then rotate the lid clockwise to lock. 6. Turn the unit on. 7. Press the SMOOTHIE BOWL button. 8. When the program is complete, turn the outer bowl and release it from the machine. 9. Transfer the smoothie into serving bowls and serve with your favorite toppings.

Serving Suggestions: Top with more honey and some granola.
Variation Tip: You can also use Greek yogurt.
Nutritional Information per Serving: Calories: 79 | Fat: 0.7g | Sat Fat: 0.2g | Carbohydrates: 16g | Fiber: 4g | Sugar: 12g | Protein: 2g

Peach and Grapefruit Smoothie Bowl

Preparation Time: 10 minutes|Servings: 2

Ingredients:

1 cup vanilla Greek yogurt
1 cup frozen peach pieces

¼ cup fresh grapefruit juice
¼ teaspoon vanilla extract
2 tablespoons honey
½ teaspoon ground cinnamon

Preparation:
1. In a high-speed blender, add all the ingredients and pulse until smooth. 2. Transfer the mixture to the Ninja CREAMi Pint. 3. Snap the lid on the pint and freeze it for 24 hours. 4. Remove the lid and assemble the unit as per the user instructions. 5. Select the SMOOTHIE BOWL program. 6. When the program is complete, remove the outer bowl. 7. Transfer the smoothie into serving bowls and serve immediately.

Serving Suggestions: Top with grapefruit slices and shredded coconut.
Variation Tip: You can also use stevia instead of honey.
Nutritional Information per Serving: Calories: 193 | Fat: 1.7g | Sat Fat: 0.3g | Carbohydrates: 35.8g |Fiber: 1.8g | Sugar: 35g | Protein: 7.9g

Blueberry Smoothie

Preparation Time: 5 Minutes|Cook Time: 10 Minutes|Serves: 1

Ingredients:

¾ cups Ocean Spray blueberry juice cocktail, chilled
⅔ cup fresh blueberries, cleaned
and rinsed
½ cup vanilla yogurt or vanilla frozen yogurt

Preparation:
1. Puree the blueberries. 2. Put the pureed blueberries, blueberry juice cocktail, and yogurt into an empty ninja CREAMi Pint 3. Place the Ninja CREAMi Pint into the outer bowl. Place the outer bowl with the Pint in it into the ninja CREAMi machine and turn until the outer bowl locks into place. Push the smoothie button. During the smoothie function, the ingredients will mix together and become very creamy. 4. Once the smoothie function has ended, turn the outer bowl and release it from the ninja CREAMi machine. 5. Scoop smoothie into a bowl.

Serving Suggestion: Serve immediately.
Variation Tip: Add fresh mint and fresh blueberries to top the smoothie.
Nutritional Information per Serving: Calories 206 | Protein 6.4g | Carbohydrate 42g | Dietary Fiber 1.5g | Sugar 17g | Fat 1.5g | Sodium 103mg

Avocado Kale Smoothie Bowl

Preparation Time: 10 minutes | Servings: 4

Ingredients:

1 banana, sliced
½ avocado, sliced
1 cup packed kale leaves

1 cup green apple, cut into pieces
¼ cup unsweetened coconut milk
2 tablespoons agave nectar

Preparation:
1. Mix all the ingredients until well combined in a large bowl. 2. Transfer the mixture into an empty Ninja CREAMi Pint. 3. Cover the pint with the lid and freeze for 24 hours. 4. After 24 hours, remove the lid and place the pint into the outer bowl of the Ninja CREAMi. 5. Install the Creamerizer Paddle onto the lid of the outer bowl, then rotate the lid clockwise to lock. 6. Turn the unit on. 7. Press the SMOOTHIE BOWL button. 8. When the program is complete, turn the outer bowl and release it from the machine. 9. Transfer the smoothie into serving bowls and serve with your favorite toppings.

Serving Suggestions: Top with nuts and fruits of your choice.
Variation Tip: You can use any milk you prefer.
Nutritional Information per Serving: Calories: 150 | Fat: 8g | Sat Fat: 4g | Carbohydrates: 19g | Fiber: 4g | Sugar: 10g | Protein: 1g

Apple Oats Smoothie Bowl

Preparation Time: 10 minutes | Cooking Time: 1 minute | Servings: 2

Ingredients:
½ cup water
¼ cup quick oats
1 cup vanilla Greek yogurt

½ cup apples, peeled and sliced
3 tablespoons honey

Preparation:
1. Put the oats and water in a microwave-safe bowl and microwave on high power for about 1 minute. 2. Remove from the microwave and stir in the yogurt, apples, and honey until well combined. 3. Transfer the mixture to the Ninja CREAMi Pint. 4. Snap the lid on the pint and freeze it for 24 hours. 5. Remove the lid and assemble the unit as per the user instructions. 6. Select the SMOOTHIE BOWL program. 7. When the program is complete, remove the outer bowl. 8. Transfer the smoothie into serving bowls and serve with your favorite toppings.

Serving Suggestions: Top with apples, sunflower seeds, and coconut flakes.
Variation Tip: You can also use maple syrup instead of honey.
Nutritional Information per Serving: Calories: 277 | Fat: 2.8g | Sat Fat: 1.1g | Carbohydrates: 55.3g | Fiber: 2.4g | Sugar: 43.1g | Protein: 10.9g

Buttery Coffee Smoothie

Preparation Time: 5 Minutes | Cook Time: 5 Minutes | Serves: 1

Ingredients:
1 cup brewed coffee
2 large pasteurized egg yolks
¼ cup avocado

¼ cup ice cubes
1 tablespoon coconut sugar
2 tablespoons coconut oil, melted

Preparation:
1. Combine the coffee, egg yolks, avocado, ice cubes, and coconut sugar in an empty ninja CREAMi Pint. 2. Place the Ninja CREAMi Pint into the outer bowl. Place the outer bowl with the Pint in it into the ninja CREAMi machine and turn until the outer bowl locks into place. Push the SMOOTHIE button. During the SMOOTHIE function, the ingredients will mix together and become very creamy. 3. Once the SMOOTHIE function has ended, turn the outer bowl and release it from the ninja CREAMi machine. 4. Scoop the smoothie into a tall glass.

Serving Suggestion: Serve immediately.
Variation Tip: Add chopped nuts of your choice.
Nutritional Information per Serving: Calories 486 | Protein 6.7g | Carbohydrate 19g | Dietary Fiber 4g | Sugar 13g | Fat 44g | Sodium 30mg

Cranberry Smoothie Bowl

Preparation Time: 10 minutes|Servings: 4

Ingredients:

½ cup oat milk
1 cup brewed coffee
2 tablespoons almond butter

1 large banana, peeled and sliced
1 cup cranberries

Preparation:

1. Put all the ingredients in a high-powered blender and pulse until smooth. 2. Transfer the mixture to the Ninja CREAMi Pint. 3. Snap the lid on the pint and freeze it for 24 hours. 4. Remove the lid and assemble the unit as per the user instructions. 5. Select the SMOOTHIE BOWL program. 6. When the program is complete, remove the outer bowl. 7. Transfer the smoothie into serving bowls and serve immediately.

Serving Suggestions: Serve with a topping of cranberries, pomegranate seeds, and granola.
Variation Tip: Cashew butter can be used instead of almond butter.
Nutritional Information per Serving: Calories: 111 | Fat: 4.9g | Sat Fat: 0.4g | Carbohydrates: 14.8g |Fiber: 2.9g | Sugar: 7.9g | Protein: 2.6g

Tropical Smoothie Bowl

Preparation Time: 10 minutes|Servings: 2

Ingredients:

1 ripe banana, cut into pieces
2 cups frozen fruit mix

1¼ cups vanilla yogurt

Preparation:

1. Mix all the ingredients until well combined in a large bowl. 2. Transfer

the mixture into an empty Ninja CREAMi Pint. 3. Cover the pint with the lid and freeze for 24 hours. 4. After 24 hours, remove the lid and place the pint into the outer bowl of the Ninja CREAMi. 5. Install the Creamerizer Paddle onto the lid of the outer bowl, then rotate the lid clockwise to lock. 6. Turn the unit on. 7. Press the SMOOTHIE BOWL button. 8. When the program is completed, turn the outer bowl and release it from the machine. 9. Transfer the smoothie into serving bowls and serve with your favorite toppings.

Serving Suggestions: Top with fresh fruits.
Variation Tip: You can also use Greek yogurt.
Nutritional Information per Serving: Calories: 71 | Fat: 0.1g | Sat Fat: 0g | Carbohydrates: 17g | Fiber: 2g | Sugar: 9g | Protein: 1g

Vodka Smoothie

Preparation Time: 5 Minutes|Cook Time: 5 Minutes|Serves: 2

Ingredients:

3 fluid ounces vodka
9 fluid ounces orange juice
½ cup frozen strawberries

2 scoops orange sherbet
½ cup crushed ice

Preparation:

1. Mix the vodka, orange juice, strawberries, orange sherbet, and ice in an empty ninja CREAMi Pint. 2. Place the Ninja CREAMi Pint into the outer bowl. Place the outer bowl with the Pint in it into the ninja CREAMi machine and turn until the outer bowl locks into place. Push the SMOOTHIE button. During the SMOOTHIE function, the ingredients will mix together and become very creamy. 3. Once the SMOOTHIE function has ended, turn the outer bowl and release it from the ninja CREAMi machine. 4. Scoop the smoothie into glass cups.

Serving Suggestion: Serve immediately.
Variation Tip: Add some fresh sliced strawberries and mint leaves.
Nutritional Information per Serving: Calories 230 | Protein 1.6g | Carbohydrate 30g | Dietary Fiber 1.4g | Sugar 27g | Fat 1.5g | Sodium 21.6mg

Vanilla Cookie Smoothie

Preparation Time: 3 Minutes|Cook Time: 5 Minutes|Serves: 2

Ingredients:
¾ cup vanilla ice cream
2 lemon cream sandwich cookies
¼ cup milk

Preparation:
1. Add the ice cream, smashed cookies, and milk to an empty ninja CREAMi Pint. 2. Place the Ninja CREAMi Pint into the outer bowl. Place the outer bowl with the Pint in it into the ninja CREAMi machine and turn until the outer bowl locks into place. Push the SMOOTHIE button. During the SMOOTHIE function, the ingredients will mix together and become very creamy. 3. Once the SMOOTHIE function has ended, turn the outer bowl and release it from the ninja CREAMi machine. 4. Pour the smoothies into tall glasses.

Serving Suggestion: Serve immediately.
Variation Tip: Add whipped cream and whole cookies on top.
Nutritional Information per Serving: Calories 237 | Protein 3g | Carbohydrate 57g | Dietary Fiber 8.4g | Sugar 34.7g | Fat 2.4g | Sodium 18.3mg

Coffee Smoothie Bowl

Preparation Time: 5 Minutes|Cook Time: 24 Hours and 5 Minutes|Serves: 1

Ingredients:
Smoothie Bowl:
1 cup coffee (brewed; not just the coffee beans or grounds)
½ cup oat milk

2 tablespoons mocha almond butter
1 cup raspberries
1 banana

Toppings:
1 banana
½ cup raspberries

1 tablespoon sliced almonds
¼ cup chocolate-covered espresso beans

1 teaspoon honey
Maple syrup

Preparation:
1. Combine all ingredients in a blender and blend until smooth. 2. Pour into an empty ninja CREAMi Pint container and freeze for 24 hours. 3. After 24 hours, remove the Pint from the freezer. Remove the lid. 4. Place the Ninja CREAMi Pint into the outer bowl. Place the outer bowl with the Pint in it into the ninja CREAMi machine and turn until the outer bowl locks into place. Push the SMOOTHIE button. During the SMOOTHIE function, the ingredients will mix together and become very creamy. 5. Once the SMOOTHIE function has ended, turn the outer bowl and release it from the ninja CREAMi machine. 6. Scoop the smoothie into a bowl. Drizzle with maple syrup or honey. Top with sliced almonds, chocolate-covered coffee beans, raspberries, and sliced bananas. 7. Your smoothie bowl is ready to eat!

Serving Suggestion: Serve immediately.
Variation Tip: Top with chocolate chips.
Nutritional Information per Serving: Calories 906 | Protein 20g | Carbohydrate 128g | Dietary Fiber 9g | Sugar 27g | Fat 41g | Sodium 79mg

Vanilla Pumpkin Pie Smoothie

Preparation Time: 10 Minutes|Cook Time: 10 Minutes|Serves: 1

Ingredients:
4 ounces pumpkin pie filling (such as Libby's)
½ cup vanilla frozen yogurt
¼ cup ice

¼ cup vanilla-flavored soy milk
½ teaspoon ground cinnamon
1 pinch ground nutmeg
⅛ teaspoon vanilla extract

Preparation:
1. Combine the pumpkin pie filling, frozen yogurt, ice, soy milk, cinnamon, nutmeg, and vanilla extract and put into an empty ninja CREAMi Pint. 2. Place the Ninja CREAMi Pint into the outer bowl. Place the outer bowl with the Pint in it into the ninja CREAMi machine and turn until the outer bowl locks into place. Push the SMOOTHIE button. During the SMOOTHIE function, the ingredients will mix together and become very creamy. 3. Once the SMOOTHIE function has ended, turn the outer bowl and release it from the ninja CREAMi machine. 4. Pour the smoothie into a glass.

Serving Suggestion: Serve immediately.
Variation Tip: Sprinkle some cinnamon and nutmeg on top.
Nutritional Information per Serving: Calories 260 | Protein 5.6g | Carbohydrate 50g | Dietary Fiber 10.3g | Sugar 20g | Fat 4.8g | Sodium 329mg

Mango & Orange Smoothie Bowl

Preparation Time: 10 minutes | Servings: 2

Ingredients:

1 cup frozen mango chunks
1 cup plain whole milk yogurt
¼ cup fresh orange juice
2 tablespoons maple syrup
½ teaspoon ground turmeric
⅛ teaspoon ground cinnamon
⅛ teaspoon ground ginger
Pinch of ground black pepper

Preparation:

1. In a high-speed blender, add all ingredients and pulse until smooth 2. Transfer the mixture into an empty Ninja CREAMi pint container. 3. Cover the container with storage lid and freeze for 24 hours. 4. After 24 hours, remove the lid from container and arrange into the Outer Bowl of Ninja CREAMi. 5. Install the Creamerizer Paddle onto the lid of Outer Bowl. 6. Then rotate the lid clockwise to lock. 7. Press Power button to turn on the unit. 8. Then press Smoothie Bowl button. 9. When the program is completed, turn the Outer Bowl and release it from the machine. 10. Transfer the smoothie into serving bowls and serve immediately.

Serving Suggestions: Serve with the toping of fresh fruit and coconut.
Variation Tip: For best result, use freshly squeezed orange juice.
Nutritional Information per Serving: Calories: 188 | Fat: 4.2g|Sat Fat: 2.5g|Carbohydrates: 34.8g|Fiber: 1.5g|Sugar: 31.1g|Protein: 4.9g

Three Fruit Smoothie Bowl

Preparation Time: 10 minutes | Servings: 2

Ingredients:

¾ cup fresh strawberries, hulled and quartered
1 cup frozen dragon fruit pieces
¾ cup pineapple, cut into 1-inch
pieces
2 tablespoons agave nectar
½ cup low-fat plain yogurt
1 tablespoon fresh lime juice

Preparation:

1. Put all the ingredients in a high-speed blender and pulse until smooth. 2. Transfer the mixture to the Ninja CREAMi Pint. 3. Snap the lid on the pint and freeze it for 24 hours. 4. Remove the lid and assemble the unit as per the user instructions. 5. Select the SMOOTHIE BOWL program. 6. When the program is complete, remove the outer bowl. 7. Transfer the smoothie into serving bowls and serve immediately.

Serving Suggestions: Top with sliced kiwi and shredded coconut.
Variation Tip: You can also use honey.
Nutritional Information per Serving: Calories: 183 | Fat: 1.2g | Sat Fat: 0.1g | Carbohydrates: 40.5g |Fiber: 4.2g | Sugar: 33.7g | Protein: 4.5g

Avocado Smoothie

Preparation Time: 5 Minutes | Cook Time: 5 Minutes | Serves: 1

Ingredients:

½ ripe avocado, peeled, halved, and pitted
½ cup milk
¼ cup vanilla yogurt
1 ½ tablespoons honey
4 ice cubes

Preparation:

1. Combine the avocado, milk, yogurt, honey, and ice cubes in an empty ninja CREAMi Pint. 2. Place the Ninja CREAMi Pint into the outer bowl. Place the outer bowl with the Pint in it into the ninja CREAMi machine and turn until the outer bowl locks into place. Push the SMOOTHIE button. During the SMOOTHIE function, the ingredients will mix together and become very creamy. 3. Once the SMOOTHIE function has ended, turn the outer bowl and release it from the ninja CREAMi machine. 4. Pour the smoothie into glasses.

Serving Suggestion: Serve immediately.
Variation Tip: Sprinkle some vanilla sugar on top.
Nutritional Information per Serving: Calories 96 | Protein 6g | Carbohydrate 18g | Dietary Fiber 0.5g | Sugar 2g | Fat 0.1g | Sodium 156mg

Apple Razzle Berry Smoothie Bowl

Preparation Time: 10 minutes|Servings: 1

Ingredients:

⅜ cup frozen apple chunks

¼ cup frozen raspberries

¼ cup whole milk Greek yogurt

⅛ cup orange juice

½ tablespoon raw agave nectar

Preparation:

1. Fill an empty Ninja CREAMi pint to the MAX FILL line with all ingredients. 2. Cover the container with a pint lid and freeze for 24 hours. 3. After 24 hours, remove the lid from the container and arrange the pint into the outer bowl of Ninja Creami. 4. Install the "Creamerizer Paddle" onto the lid of the outer bowl. 5. Then rotate the lid clockwise to lock. 6. Turn on the unit. 7. Then select the "SMOOTHIE BOWL" function. 8. When the program is completed, turn the outer bowl and release it from the machine. 9. Transfer the smoothie into serving bowls and serve with your favorite topping.

Serving Suggestions: Top with apple chunks.

Variation Tip: You can also use honey.

Nutritional Information per Serving: Calories: 178 | Fat: 2.6g| Sat Fat: 0.4g| Carbohydrates: 39g| Fiber: 4g| Sugar: 33g| Protein: 1.3g

Fruity Coconut Smoothie Bowl

Preparation Time: 10 minutes|Servings: 1

Ingredients:

½ cup coconut milk

¼ frozen berries

1 frozen banana

1 tablespoon sugar

Preparation:

1. Fill an empty Ninja CREAMi pint to the MAX FILL line with all ingredients. 2. Cover the container with a pint lid and freeze for 24 hours. 3. After 24 hours, remove the lid from the container and arrange it into the outer bowl of Ninja Creami. 4. Install the "Creamerizer Paddle" onto the lid of the outer bowl. 5. Then rotate the lid clockwise to lock. 6. Turn on the unit. 7. Then select the "SMOOTHIE BOWL" function. 8. When the program is completed, turn the outer bowl and release it from the machine. 9. Transfer the smoothie into serving bowls and serve with your favorite topping.

Serving Suggestions: Top with banana slices.

Variation Tip: You can also use honey.

Nutritional Information per Serving: Calories: 278 | Fat: 24g| Sat Fat: 21g| Carbohydrates: 7g| Fiber: 3g| Sugar: 4.3g| Protein: 2.3g

Peaches Smoothie Bowl

Preparation Time: 5 minutes|Servings: 1

Ingredients:

½ cup whole milk

½ cup frozen strawberries

1 frozen peaches

1 tablespoon sugar

Preparation:

1. Fill an empty Ninja CREAMi pint to the MAX FILL line with all ingredients. 2. Cover the container with a pint lid and freeze for 24 hours. 3. After 24 hours, remove the lid from the container and arrange it into the outer bowl of Ninja Creami. 4. Install the "Creamerizer Paddle" onto the lid of the outer bowl. 5. Then rotate the lid clockwise to lock. 6. Turn on the unit. 7. Then select the "SMOOTHIE BOWL" function. 8. When the program is completed, turn the outer bowl and release it from the machine. 9. Transfer the smoothie into serving bowls and serve with your favorite topping.

Serving Suggestions: Top with peach slices.

Variation Tip: You can also use honey instead of sugar.

Nutritional Information per Serving: Calories: 256 | Fat: 6.3g| Sat Fat: 4.1g| Carbohydrates: 43g| Fiber: 2.2g| Sugar: 37g| Protein: 3.2g

Grapefruit Smoothie Bowl

Preparation Time: 5 minutes|Servings: 1

Ingredients:

2 cups frozen berries
½ cup grapefruit juice

1 tablespoon sugar

Preparation:

1. Fill an empty Ninja Creami pint to the MAX FILL line with all ingredients. 2. Cover the container with a pint lid and freeze for 24 hours. 3. After 24 hours, remove the lid from the container and arrange it into the outer bowl of Ninja Creami. 4. Install the "Creamerizer Paddle" onto the lid of the outer bowl. 5. Then rotate the lid clockwise to lock. 6. Turn on the unit. 7. Then select the "SMOOTHIE BOWL" function. 8. When the program is completed, turn the outer bowl and release it from the machine. 9. Transfer the smoothie into serving bowls and serve with your favorite topping.

Serving Suggestions: Top with berries.
Variation Tip: You can use any sweetener.
Nutritional Information per Serving: Calories: 102 | Fat: 0.1g| Sat Fat: 0g| Carbohydrates: 30g| Fiber: 5g| Sugar: 22g| Protein: 1.2g

Orange Cranberries Smoothie Bowl

Preparation Time: 5 minutes|Servings: 1

Ingredients:

1 cup fresh cranberries
¼ cup vanilla yogurt

⅛ cup orange juice
1 tablespoon sugar

Preparation:

1. Fill an empty Ninja CREAMi pint to the MAX FILL line with all ingredients. 2. Cover the container with a pint lid and freeze for 24 hours. 3. After 24 hours, remove the lid from the container and arrange it into the outer bowl of Ninja Creami. 4. Install the "Creamerizer Paddle" onto the lid of the outer bowl. 5. Then rotate the lid clockwise to lock. 6. Turn on the unit. 7. Then select the "SMOOTHIE BOWL" function. 8. When the program is completed, turn the outer bowl and release it from the machine. 9. Transfer the smoothie into serving bowls and serve with your favorite topping.

Serving Suggestions: Top with fruit slices.
Variation Tip: You can use any sweetener.
Nutritional Information per Serving: Calories: 233 | Fat: 1.1g| Sat Fat: 0.5g| Carbohydrates: 56g| Fiber: 0.4g| Sugar: 54g| Protein: 4g

Coconut Berries Smoothie Bowl

Preparation Time: 5 minutes|Servings: 2

Ingredients:

1 cup frozen berries
⅛ cup frozen sliced strawberries
⅛ cup pineapple juice

⅛ cup raw agave nectar
⅛ cup unsweetened coconut milk

Preparation:

1. Combine berries, sliced strawberries, pineapple juice, agave nectar, and coconut milk in a blender and blend until fully smooth. 2. Fill an empty Ninja Creami pint to the MAX FILL line with mixture. 3. Cover the container with a pint lid and freeze for 24 hours. 4. After 24 hours, remove the lid from the container and arrange it into the outer bowl of Ninja Creami. 5. Install the "Creamerizer Paddle" onto the lid of the outer bowl. 6. Then rotate the lid clockwise to lock. 7. Turn on the unit. 8. Then select the "SMOOTHIE BOWL" function. 9. When the program is completed, turn the outer bowl and release it from the machine. 10. Transfer the smoothie into serving bowls and serve with your favorite topping.

Serving Suggestions: Top with fruit slices.
Variation Tip: You can use any sweetener.
Nutritional Information per Serving: Calories: 74 | Fat: 3g| Sat Fat: 3.2g| Carbohydrates: 10g| Fiber: 1.2g| Sugar: 8g| Protein: 0.6g

Fruity Coconut Smoothie Bowl

Preparation Time: 10 minutes|Servings: 2

Ingredients:
¼ cup coconut rum
½ ripe banana, peeled and cut into
½-inch pieces
¼ cup unsweetened coconut cream
¾ cup pineapple juice
½ cup unsweetened canned coconut milk
2 tablespoons fresh lime juice

Preparation:
1. Put the banana along with the remaining ingredients in a large-sized bowl and beat until well blended. 2. Transfer the mixture to the Ninja CREAMi Pint. 3. Snap the lid on the pint and freeze it for 24 hours. 4. Remove the lid and assemble the unit as per the user instructions. 5. Select the SMOOTHIE BOWL program. 6. When the program is complete, remove the outer bowl. 7. Transfer the smoothie into serving bowls and serve immediately.

Serving Suggestions: Top with granola, banana slices, and shredded coconut.
Variation Tip: You can use almond cream instead of coconut cream.
Nutritional Information per Serving: Calories: 232 | Fat: 8.5g | Sat Fat: 3.1g | Carbohydrates: 20.5g |Fiber: 1g | Sugar: 14.5g | Protein: 1.4g

Fruity Avocado Smoothie Bowl

Preparation Time: 5 minutes|Servings: 2

Ingredients:
1 cup avocado
⅛ cup frozen pineapple chunks
⅛ cup orange juice
⅛ cup raw agave nectar
⅛ cup coconut milk

Preparation:
1. Combine avocado, pineapple chunks, orange juice, agave nectar, and coconut milk in a blender and blend until fully smooth. 2. Fill an empty Ninja Creami pint to the MAX FILL line with mixture. 3. Cover the container with a pint lid and freeze for 24 hours. 4. After 24 hours, remove the lid from the container and arrange it into the outer bowl of Ninja Creami. 5. Install the "Creamerizer Paddle" onto the lid of the outer bowl. 6. Then rotate the lid clockwise to lock. 7. Turn on the unit. 8. Then select the "SMOOTHIE BOWL" function. 9. When the program is completed, turn the outer bowl and release it from the machine. 10. Transfer the smoothie into serving bowls and serve with your favorite topping.

Serving Suggestions: Top with fruit slices.
Variation Tip: You can use any sweetener.
Nutritional Information per Serving: Calories: 57 | Fat: 3.7g| Sat Fat: 3g| Carbohydrates: 6g| Fiber: 0.6g| Sugar: 5g| Protein: 0.6g

Pumpkin Smoothie Bowl

Preparation Time: 10 minutes|Servings: 2

Ingredients:
1 cup canned pumpkin puree
⅓ cup plain Greek yogurt
1½ tablespoons maple syrup
1 teaspoon vanilla extract
1 teaspoon pumpkin pie spice
1 frozen banana, peeled and cut in ½-inch pieces

Preparation:
1. In an empty Ninja CREAMi pint container, add the pumpkin puree, yogurt, maple syrup, vanilla extract and pumpkin pie spice and mix well. 2. Add the banana pieces and stir to combine. 3. Transfer the mixture into an empty Ninja CREAMi pint container. 4. Arrange the container into the Outer Bowl of Ninja CREAMi. 5. Install the Creamerizer Paddle onto the lid of Outer Bowl. 6. Then rotate the lid clockwise to lock. 7. Press Power button to turn on the unit. 8. Then press Smoothie Bowl button. 9. When the program is completed, turn the Outer Bowl and release it from the machine. 10. Transfer the smoothie into serving bowls and serve immediately.

Serving Suggestions: Serve with garnishing of pumpkin seeds and chocolate chips.
Variation Tip: Use sugar-free pumpkin puree.
Nutritional Information per Serving: Calories: 170 | Fat: 0.7g|Sat Fat: 0.3g|Carbohydrates: 35.8g|Fiber: 5.2g|Sugar: 22g|Protein: 7.5g

Pineapple Strawberry Smoothie Bowl

Preparation Time: 5 minutes|Servings: 2

Ingredients:

1 cup frozen sliced strawberries
⅜ cup pineapple juice

1 ½ tablespoons honey

Preparation:

1. Fill an empty Ninja Creami pint to the MAX FILL line with all ingredients. 2. Cover the container with a pint lid and freeze for 24 hours. 3. After 24 hours, remove the lid from the container and arrange it into the outer bowl of Ninja Creami. 4. Install the "Creamerizer Paddle" onto the lid of the outer bowl. 5. Then rotate the lid clockwise to lock. 6. Turn on the unit. 7. Then select the "SMOOTHIE BOWL" function. 8. When the program is completed, turn the outer bowl and release it from the machine. 9. Transfer the smoothie into serving bowls and serve with your favorite topping.

Serving Suggestions: Top with fruit slices.
Variation Tip: You can use any sweetener.
Nutritional Information per Serving: Calories: 27 | Fat: 0.1g| Sat Fat: 0g| Carbohydrates: 6.2g| Fiber: 0.1g| Sugar: 4g| Protein: 0.2g

Cherries Almond Smoothie Bowl

Preparation Time: 5 minutes|Servings: 1

Ingredients:

½ cup almond milk
3 tablespoons cocoa powder

honey, as desired
frozen cherries, as desired

Preparation:

1. Fill an empty Ninja Creami pint to the MAX FILL line with all ingredients. 2. Cover the container with a pint lid and freeze for 24 hours. 3. After 24 hours, remove the lid from the container and arrange it into the outer bowl of Ninja Creami. 4. Install the "Creamerizer Paddle" onto the lid of the outer bowl. 5. Then rotate the lid clockwise to lock. 6. Turn on the unit. 7. Then select the "SMOOTHIE BOWL" function. 8. When the program is completed, turn the outer bowl and release it from the machine. 9. Transfer the smoothie into serving bowls and serve with your favorite topping.

Serving Suggestions: Top with almond slices.
Variation Tip: You can use any sweetener.
Nutritional Information per Serving: Calories: 315 | Fat: 30g| Sat Fat: 23g| Carbohydrates: 16g| Fiber: 7g| Sugar: 5g| Protein: 5g

Maple Pumpkin Smoothie Bowl

Preparation Time: 5 minutes|Servings: 2

Ingredients:

1 cup canned pumpkin puree
⅓ cup yogurt of choice

1 ½ tablespoons maple syrup
1 teaspoon vanilla extract

Preparation:

1. Fill an empty Ninja CREAMi pint to the MAX FILL line with all ingredients. 2. Cover the container with a pint lid and freeze for 24 hours. 3. After 24 hours, remove the lid from the container and arrange it into the outer bowl of Ninja Creami. 4. Install the "Creamerizer Paddle" onto the lid of the outer bowl. 5. Then rotate the lid clockwise to lock. 6. Turn on the unit. 7. Then select the "SMOOTHIE BOWL" function. 8. When the program is completed, turn the outer bowl and release it from the machine. 9. Transfer the smoothie into serving bowls and serve with your favorite topping.

Serving Suggestions: Top with banana slices.
Variation Tip: You can use honey.
Nutritional Information per Serving: Calories: 111 | Fat: 1.9g| Sat Fat: 0.9g| Carbohydrates: 19.9g| Fiber: 1.4g| Sugar: 14g| Protein: 2.8g

Lime Coconut Smoothie Bowl

Preparation Time: 5 minutes|Servings: 1

Ingredients:
¼ cup unsweetened coconut cream
½ cup unsweetened canned coconut milk
¾ cup pineapple juice
2 tablespoons lime juice

Preparation:
1. Fill an empty Ninja Creami pint to the MAX FILL line with all ingredients. 2. Cover the container with a pint lid and freeze for 24 hours. 3. After 24 hours, remove the lid from the container and arrange it into the outer bowl of Ninja Creami. 4. Install the "Creamerizer Paddle" onto the lid of the outer bowl. 5. Then rotate the lid clockwise to lock. 6. Turn on the unit. 7. Then select the "SMOOTHIE BOWL" function. 8. When the program is completed, turn the outer bowl and release it from the machine. 9. Transfer the smoothie into serving bowls and serve with your favorite topping.

Serving Suggestions: Top with nuts.
Variation Tip: You can use Macadamia nuts.
Nutritional Information per Serving: Calories: 617 | Fat: 34g| Sat Fat: 29g| Carbohydrates: 54g| Fiber: 2g| Sugar: 25g| Protein: 7g

Carrot Vanilla Smoothie Bowl

Preparation Time: 5 minutes|Servings: 1

Ingredients:
½ cup whole milk
1 frozen banana, quartered
½ cup frozen carrots
¼ cup rolled oats
2 tablespoons vanilla Greek yogurt
½ teaspoon cinnamon

Preparation:
1. Fill an empty Ninja Creami pint to the MAX FILL line with all ingredients. 2. Cover the container with a pint lid and freeze for 24 hours. 3. After 24 hours, remove the lid from the container and arrange it into the outer bowl of Ninja Creami. 4. Install the "Creamerizer Paddle" onto the lid of the outer bowl. 5. Then rotate the lid clockwise to lock. 6. Turn on the unit. 7. Then select the "SMOOTHIE BOWL" function. 8. When the program is completed, turn the outer bowl and release it from the machine. 9. Transfer the smoothie into serving bowls and serve with your favorite topping.

Serving Suggestions: Sprinkle cinnamon on top.
Variation Tip: You can also top with chia seeds.
Nutritional Information per Serving: Calories: 517 | Fat: 44g| Sat Fat: 39g| Carbohydrates: 34g| Fiber: 9g| Sugar: 13g| Protein: 11g

Yogurt Strawberries Smoothie Bowl

Preparation Time: 5 minutes|Servings: 4

Ingredients:
1 cup frozen pitaya pieces
¾ cup fresh strawberries
¾ cup pineapple, cut in 1-inch
pieces
½ cup low fat plain yogurt
2 tablespoons honey

Preparation:
1. Combine all ingredients in a blender and blend until fully smooth. 2. Fill an empty CREAMi pint to the MAX FILL line with mixture. 3. Cover the container with a pint lid and freeze for 24 hours. 4. After 24 hours, remove the lid from the container and arrange it into the outer bowl of Ninja Creami. 5. Install the "Creamerizer Paddle" onto the lid of the outer bowl. 6. Then rotate the lid clockwise to lock. 7. Turn on the unit. 8. Then select the "SMOOTHIE BOWL" function. 9. When the program is completed, turn the outer bowl and release it from the machine. 10. Transfer the smoothie into serving bowls and serve with your favorite topping.

Serving Suggestions: Top with berries.
Variation Tip: You can also top with pineapple chunks.
Nutritional Information per Serving: Calories: 143 | Fat: 2g| Sat Fat: 1g| Carbohydrates: 29.6g| Fiber: 1g| Sugar: 27.5g| Protein: 3.3g

Caramel Corn Ice Cream

Preparation Time: 10 minutes | Servings: 6

Ingredients:

½ cup butterscotch pieces, chopped
¾ cup caramel corn, roughly chopped
1 cup whole milk
¾ cup heavy cream
⅓ cup granulated sugar

Preparation:

1. Add the ingredients to a blender. Mix well until smooth. 2. Pour the mixture into the Ninja CREAMi Pint and close it with the lid. 3. Place the pint into the freezer and freeze for 24 hours. 4. Once done, open the lid, place the pint into the outer bowl of the Ninja CREAMi, and set the Creamerizer Paddle into the outer bowl. 5. Lock the lid by rotating it clockwise. 6. Turn on the unit and press the ICE CREAM button. 7. Once done, take out the bowl from the Ninja CREAMi. 8. Serve and enjoy.

Serving Suggestions: Serve with caramel sauce on top.
Variation Tip: You can add raw honey to enhance the taste.
Nutritional Information per Serving: Calories: 185 | Fat: 10.2g | Sat Fat: 6.7g | Carbohydrates: 21g | Fiber: 0g | Sugar: 20.8g | Protein: 2.5g

Fruity Cereal Ice Cream

Preparation Time: 30 Minutes | Cook Time: 24 Hours and 30 Minutes | Serves: 2

Ingredients:

¾ cup whole milk
1 cup fruity cereal, divided
1 tablespoon Philadelphia cream cheese, softened
¼ cup granulated sugar
1 teaspoon vanilla extract
½ cup heavy cream

Preparation:

1. In a large mixing bowl, combine ½ cup of the fruity cereal and the milk. Allow the mixture to settle for 15–30 minutes, stirring occasionally to infuse the milk with the fruity taste. 2. Microwave the Philadelphia cream cheese for 10 seconds in a second large microwave-safe dish. Combine the sugar and vanilla extract in a mixing bowl with a whisk or rubber spatula until the mixture resembles frosting, about 60 seconds. 3. After 15 to 30 minutes, sift the milk and cereal into the bowl with the sugar mixture using a fine-mesh filter. To release extra milk, press on the cereal with a spoon, then discard it. Mix in the heavy cream until everything is thoroughly mixed. 4. Pour the mixture into an empty ninja CREAMi Pint container. Add the strawberries to the Pint, making sure not to go over the max fill line, and freeze for 24 hours. 5. After 24 hours, remove the Pint from the freezer. Remove the lid. 6. Place the Ninja CREAMi Pint into the outer bowl. Place the outer bowl with the Pint in it into the ninja CREAMi machine and turn until the outer bowl locks into place. Push the ICE CREAM button. During the ICE CREAM function, the ice cream will mix together and become very creamy. 7. Use a spoon to create a 1½-inch wide hole that reaches the bottom of the Pint. Add the remaining ½ cup of fruity cereal to the hole and process again using the mix-in. When processing is complete, remove the ice cream from the Pint.

Serving Suggestion: Serve immediately.
Variation Tip: Add fruit of your choice.
Nutritional Information per Serving: Calories 140 | Protein 0.5g | Carbohydrate 25g | Dietary Fiber 0.5g | Sugar 20g | Fat 2g | Sodium 46mg

Chocolate Peppermint Ice Cream

Preparation Time: 5 minutes|Servings: 4

Ingredients:
½ cup frozen kale, thawed and squeezed dry
½ cup dark brown sugar
1 cup whole milk
1 teaspoon peppermint extract
3 tablespoons dark cocoa powder
⅓ cup heavy cream
8 striped peppermint candies, roughly chopped

Preparation:
1. In a blender pitcher, combine the kale, sugar, milk, peppermint extract, and cocoa powder. Blend on high for 60 seconds or until the mixture is perfectly smooth. 2. Transfer the mixture to the Ninja CREAMi Pint. 3. Snap the lid on the pint and freeze it for 24 hours. 4. Remove the lid and assemble the unit as per the user instructions. 5. Select the ICE CREAM program. 6. When the program is completed, use a spoon to create a 1½-inch wide hole in the center of the ice cream that reaches the bottom of the pint. 7. Add the chopped peppermint candy pieces to the hole and select the MIX-IN program. 8. When the program is complete, remove the outer bowl. 9. Serve in bowls.

Serving Suggestions: Garnish with chocolate chips.
Variation Tip: You can also use fresh kale.
Nutritional Information per Serving: Calories: 148 | Fat: 5g | Sat Fat: 3g | Carbohydrates: 22g |Fiber: 0.3g | Sugar: 20g | Protein: 2g

Grasshopper Ice Cream

Preparation Time: 15 minutes|Servings: 4

Ingredients:
½ cup frozen spinach, thawed and   squeezed dry

1 cup whole milk
½ cup granulated sugar
1 teaspoon mint extract
3-5 drops green food coloring
⅓ cup heavy cream
¼ cup chocolate chunks, chopped
¼ cup brownie, cut into 1-inch pieces

Preparation:
1. In a high-speed blender, add the spinach, milk, sugar, mint extract and food coloring and pulse until mixture smooth. 2. Transfer the mixture into an empty Ninja CREAMi pint container. 3. Add the heavy cream and stir until well combined. 4. Cover the container with storage lid and freeze for 24 hours. 5. After 24 hours, remove the lid from container and arrange into the Outer Bowl of Ninja CREAMi. 6. Install the Creamerizer Paddle onto the lid of Outer Bowl. 7. Then rotate the lid clockwise to lock. 8. Press Power button to turn on the unit. 9. Then press Ice Cream button. 10. When the program is completed, with a spoon, create a 1½-inch wide hole in the center that reaches the bottom of the pint container. 11. Add the chocolate chunks and brownie pieces into the hole and press Mix-In button. 12. When the program is completed, turn the Outer Bowl and release it from the machine. 13. Transfer the ice cream into serving bowls and serve immediately.

Serving Suggestions: Serve with the garnishing of chocolate shaving.
Variation Tip: Make sure to squeeze the spinach completely.
Nutritional Information per Serving: Calories: 243 | Fat: 10.1g|Sat Fat: 6g|Carbohydrates: 36.7g|Fiber: 0.4g|Sugar: 33.7g|Protein: 3.4g

Lite Chocolate Cookie Ice Cream

Preparation Time: 5 Minutes|Cook Time: 24 Hours and 5 Minutes|Serves: 2

Ingredients:
1 tablespoon cream cheese, at room temperature
2 tablespoons unsweetened cocoa powder
½ teaspoon stevia sweetener
3 tablespoons raw agave nectar
1 teaspoon vanilla extract
¾ cup heavy cream
1 cup whole milk
¼ cup crushed reduced-fat sugar cookies

Preparation:
1. Place the cream cheese in a large microwave-safe bowl and heat on high for 10 seconds. 2. Mix in the cocoa powder, stevia, agave, and vanilla. Microwave for 60 seconds more, or until the mixture resembles frosting. 3. Slowly whisk in the heavy cream and milk until the sugar has dissolved and the mixture is thoroughly mixed. 4. Pour the base into a clean CREAMi Pint. Place the storage lid on the container and freeze for 24 hours. 5. Remove the Pint from the freezer and take off the lid. Place the Pint in the outer bowl of your Ninja CREAMi, install the Creamerizer Paddle in the outer bowl lid, and lock the lid assembly onto the outer bowl. Place the bowl assembly on the motor base, and twist the handle to the right to raise the platform and lock it in place. Select the LITE ICE CREAM function. 6. Once the machine has finished processing, remove the lid. With a spoon, create a 1½-inch-wide hole that reaches the bottom of the Pint. During this process, it's okay if your treat goes above the max fill line. Add the crushed cookies to the hole in the Pint. Replace the Pint lid and select the MIX-IN function. 7. Once the machine has finished processing, remove the ice cream from the Pint.

Serving Suggestion: Serve immediately.
Variation Tip: Add cinnamon if you like.
Nutritional Information per Serving: Calories 150 | Protein 5g | Carbohydrate 25g | Dietary Fiber 1g | Sugar 19g | Fat 4g | Sodium 65mg

Maple Walnut Ice Cream

Preparation Time: 10 minutes|Servings: 4

Ingredients:

1 tablespoon cream cheese, softened

⅓ cup granulated sugar

1 teaspoon maple extract

¾ cup heavy cream

1 cup whole milk

¼ cup walnuts, chopped, for mix-in

Preparation:

1. Microwave the cream cheese for 10 seconds in a large microwave-safe bowl. Add the sugar and maple extract and combine with a whisk or rubber spatula for about 60 seconds, or until the mixture forms frosting. 2. Slowly whisk in the heavy cream and milk until smooth, and the sugar has dissolved. 3. Transfer the mixture to the Ninja CREAMi Pint. 4. Snap the lid on the pint and freeze it for 24 hours. 5. Remove the lid and assemble the unit as per the user instructions. 6. Select the ICE CREAM program. 7. When the program is complete, use a spoon to create a 1½-inch wide hole in the center of the ice cream that reaches the bottom of the pint. 8. Add the chopped walnuts to the hole and select the MIX-IN program. 9. When the program is complete, remove the outer bowl. 10. Serve in bowls.

Serving Suggestions: Top with walnuts.
Variation Tip: You can also use soy milk.
Nutritional Information per Serving: Calories: 237 | Fat: 15g | Sat Fat: 7g | Carbohydrates: 21g |Fiber: 0.5g | Sugar: 20g | Protein: 4g

Wafer Lavender Ice Cream

Preparation Time: 20 minutes|Servings: 4

Ingredients:

¾ cup cream

1 tablespoon dried culinary lavender

⅛ teaspoon kosher salt

¾ cup whole milk

½ cup sweetened condensed milk

⅓ cup crushed chocolate wafer cookies

Preparation:

1. Combine heavy cream, lavender, and salt in a medium pot. To combine the ingredients, whisk them together. 2. Steep for 10 minutes in a pot over low heat, stirring every 2 minutes to prevent bubbling. 3. Drain lavender from heavy cream into a large mixing bowl using a fine-mesh strainer. Discard lavender. 4. Combine the milk and sweetened condensed milk in a large mixing basin. Whisk until the mixture is completely smooth. 5. Transfer the mixture into a Ninja Creami pint. 6. Cover the container with a pint lid and freeze for 24 hours. 7. After 24 hours, remove the lid from the container and arrange it into the outer bowl of Ninja Creami. 8. Install the "Creamerizer Paddle" onto the lid of the outer bowl. 9. Then rotate the lid clockwise to lock. 10. Turn on the unit. 11. Then select the "ICE CREAM" function. 12. When the program is completed, with a spoon, create a 1½-inch wide hole in the center that reaches the bottom of the pint. 13. Add crushed wafer cookies to the hole and select the "MIX-IN" function. 14. When the program is completed, turn the outer bowl and release it from the machine. 15. Serve in bowls.

Serving Suggestions: Top with crushed cookies.
Variation Tip: You can use any flavored cookies.
Nutritional Information per Serving: Calories: 268 | Fat: 14g| Sat Fat: 8g| Carbohydrates: 30g| Fiber: 0g| Sugar: 26g| Protein: 5g

Orange Chunk Chocolate Ice Cream

Preparation Time: 10 minutes|Servings: 2

Ingredients:

2 tablespoons orange zest, grated

1 cup white chocolate, chopped

1 cup whole milk

¾ cup heavy cream

2 tablespoons mini chocolate chips

2 tablespoons cocoa powder

⅓ cup granulated sugar

Preparation:

1. Place all the ingredients in a blender. Mix well until smooth. 2. Pour the mixture into the Ninja CREAMi Pint and close the lid. 3. Place the pint into the freezer and freeze for 24 hours. 4. Once done, open the lid and place the pint into the outer bowl of the Ninja CREAMi. Set the Creamerizer Paddle into the outer bowl. 5. Lock the lid by rotating it clockwise. 6. Turn the unit on and press the ICE CREAM button. 7. Once done, take out the bowl from the Ninja CREAMi. 8. Serve and enjoy your delicious ice cream.

Serving Suggestions: Serve with some white chocolate chips on top.
Variation Tip: You can skip the chocolate chips.
Nutritional Information per Serving: Calories: 929 | Fat: 53.1g | Sat Fat: 32.1g | Carbohydrates: 108.9g | Fiber: 2.4g | Sugar: 97g | Protein: 11.9g

Jelly Ice Cream

Preparation Time: 25 minutes|Servings: 4

Ingredients:

4 large egg yolks
3 tablespoons granulated sugar
⅓ cup heavy cream
1 cup whole milk

¼ cup smooth peanut butter
3 tablespoons grape jelly
¼ cup honey roasted peanuts, chopped, for mix-in

Preparation:

1. Combine the egg yolks and sugar in a small saucepan over medium heat. Whisk until everything is well blended and the sugar has dissolved. 2. Add the heavy cream, milk, peanut butter, and grape jelly. Stir to combine. 3. Stir continuously until the mixture reaches a temperature of 165°F–175°F. 4. Remove the mixture from the heat, let it cool, and transfer it to the Ninja CREAMi Pint. 5. Snap the lid on the pint and freeze it for 24 hours. 6. Remove the lid and assemble the unit as per the user instructions. 7. Select the ICE CREAM program. 8. When the program is complete, create a 1½-inch wide hole using a spoon in the center of the ice cream that reaches the bottom of the pint. 9. Add the honey-roasted peanuts to the hole and select the MIX-IN program. 10. When the program is complete, remove the outer bowl. 11. Serve in bowls.

Serving Suggestions: Top with some jelly.
Variation Tip: You can use any flavor of jelly.
Nutritional Information per Serving: Calories: 340 | Fat: 22g | Sat Fat: 7g | Carbohydrates: 26g |Fiber: 1g | Sugar: 20g | Protein: 11g

Pistachio Ice Cream

Preparation Time: 5 Minutes|Cook Time: 24 Hours and 5 Minutes|Serves: 4

Ingredients:

1 tablespoon cream cheese, softened
⅓ cup granulated sugar
1 teaspoon almond extract
¾ cup heavy cream

1 cup whole milk
Green food coloring (optional)
¼ cup pistachios (shells removed, chopped)

Preparation:

1. Microwave the cream cheese for 10 seconds in a large microwave-safe bowl. 2. With a whisk or rubber spatula, blend in the sugar and almond extract until the mixture resembles frosting, about 60 seconds. 3. Slowly whisk in the heavy cream, milk, and optional food coloring until thoroughly mixed and the sugar has dissolved. 4. Pour the base into an empty CREAMi Pint. Place the storage lid on the Pint and freeze for 24 hours. 5. Remove the Pint from the freezer and remove its lid. Place the Pint in the outer bowl, install the Creamerizer Paddle onto the outer bowl lid, and lock the lid assembly on the outer bowl. Select ICE CREAM. 6. With a spoon, create a 1½-inch wide hole that reaches the bottom of the Pint. During this process, it's okay for your treat to press above the max fill line. Add the pistachios to the hole and process again using the MIX-IN program. 7. When processing is complete, remove the ice cream from the Pint.

Serving Suggestion: Serve immediately.
Variation Tip: Sprinkle cinnamon over the top if you like!
Nutritional Information per Serving: Calories 190 | Protein 3g | Carbohydrate 16g | Dietary Fiber 1g | Sugar 12g | Fat 13g | Sodium 40mg

Vanilla Pecan Ice Cream

Preparation Time: 10 minutes|Servings: 6

Ingredients:

1 cup whole milk
¾ cup heavy cream
⅓ cup granulated sugar
½ cup toasted pecans, coarsely

chopped
5 pecan shortbread cookies
½ cup potato chips, crushed

Preparation:

1. Place all the ingredients in a blender. Mix well until smooth. 2. Pour the mixture into the Ninja CREAMi Pint and close it with the lid. 3. Place the pint into the freezer and freeze for 24 hours. 4. Once done, remove the lid and place the pint into the outer bowl of the Ninja CREAMi. Secure the Creamerizer Paddle into the outer bowl. 5. Lock the lid by rotating it clockwise. 6. Turn on the unit and press the ICE CREAM button. 7. Once done, take out the bowl from the Ninja CREAMi. 8. Serve and enjoy.

Serving Suggestions: Serve with caramel sauce on top.
Variation Tip: You can also add some raw honey to enhance the taste.
Nutritional Information per Serving: Calories: 209 | Fat: 11.1g | Sat Fat: 5.3g | Carbohydrates: 24.8g | Fiber: 0.2g | Sugar: 16.8g | Protein: 2.7g

Banana and Chocolate Chunk Ice Cream

Preparation Time: 10 minutes | Servings: 4

Ingredients:

1 tablespoon (½ ounce) cream cheese, softened
⅓ cup granulated sugar
1 teaspoon banana extract
¾ cup heavy cream

1 cup whole milk
2 tablespoons chocolate chunks, for mix-in
2 tablespoons walnuts, for mix-in

Preparation:

1. Microwave the cream cheese for 10 seconds in a large microwave-safe bowl. Add the sugar and banana extract and combine with a whisk for about 60 seconds. 2. Slowly whisk in the heavy cream and milk until smooth, and the sugar has dissolved. 3. Transfer the mixture to the Ninja CREAMi Pint. 4. Snap the lid on the pint and freeze it for 24 hours. 5. After 24 hours, remove the lid from the container and arrange it into the outer bowl of Ninja CREAMi. 6. Remove the lid and assemble the unit as per the user instructions. 7. Select the ICE CREAM program. 8. When the program is complete, create a 1½-inch wide hole in the center of the ice cream with a spoon that reaches the bottom of the pint. 9. Add the chocolate chunks and walnuts to the hole and select the MIX-IN program. 10. When the program is complete, remove the outer bowl. 11. Serve in bowls.

Serving Suggestions: Top with chopped nuts.
Variation Tip: You can use dark, milk, or white chocolate.
Nutritional Information per Serving: Calories: 213 | Fat: 13g | Sat Fat: 7g | Carbohydrates: 20g | Fiber: 0.3g | Sugar: 20g | Protein: 3g

Chocolate Brownie Ice Cream

Preparation Time: 14 minutes | Servings: 4

Ingredients:

1 tablespoon cream cheese, softened
⅓ cup granulated sugar
1 teaspoon vanilla extract

2 tablespoons cocoa powder
1 cup whole milk
¾ cup heavy cream
2 tablespoons mini chocolate chips

2 tablespoons brownie chunks

Preparation:

1. In a large microwave-safe bowl, add the cream cheese and microwave on High for about ten seconds. 2. Remove from the microwave and stir until smooth. 3. Add the sugar and almond extract and with a wire whisk, beat until the mixture looks like frosting. 4. Slowly add the milk and heavy cream and beat until well combined. 5. Transfer the mixture into an empty Ninja CREAMi pint container. 6. Cover the container with storage lid and freeze for 24 hours. 7. After 24 hours, remove the lid from container and arrange into the Outer Bowl of Ninja CREAMi. 8. Install the Creamerizer Paddle onto the lid of Outer Bowl. 9. Then rotate the lid clockwise to lock. 10. Press Power button to turn on the unit. 11. Then press Ice Cream button. 12. When the program is completed, with a spoon, create a 1½-inch wide hole in the center that reaches the bottom of the pint container. 13. Add the chocolate chunks and brownie pieces into the hole and press Mix-In button. 14. When the program is completed, turn the Outer Bowl and release it from the machine. 15. Transfer the ice cream into serving bowls and serve immediately.

Serving Suggestions: Serve with the topping of cherries.
Variation Tip: Use high-quality cocoa powder.
Nutritional Information per Serving: Calories: 232 | Fat: 13.7g | Sat Fat: 8.3g | Carbohydrates: 25.9g | Fiber: 1g | Sugar: 22.8g | Protein: 3.6g

Jelly & Peanut Butter Ice Cream

Preparation Time: 15 minutes | Cooking Time: 5 minutes | Servings: 4

Ingredients:

3 tablespoons granulated sugar
4 large egg yolks
1 cup whole milk
⅓ cup heavy cream

¼ cup smooth peanut butter
3 tablespoons grape jelly
¼ cup honey roasted peanuts, chopped

Preparation:

1. In a small saucepan, add the sugar and egg yolks and beat until sugar is dissolved. 2. Add the milk, heavy cream, peanut butter, and grape jelly to the saucepan and stir to combine. 3. Place saucepan over medium heat and cook until temperature reaches cook until temperature reaches to 165 -175° F, stirring continuously with a rubber spatula. 4. Remove from the heat and through a fine-mesh strainer, strain the mixture into an empty Ninja CREAMi pint container. 5. Place the container into ice bath to cool. 6. After cooling, cover the container with storage lid and freeze for 24 hours. 7. After 24 hours, remove the lid from container and arrange into the Outer Bowl of Ninja CREAMi. 8. Install the Creamerizer Paddle onto the lid of Outer Bowl. 9. Then rotate the lid clockwise to lock. 10. Press Power button to turn on the unit. 11. Then press ICE CREAM button. 12. When the program is completed, with a spoon, create a 1½-inch wide hole in the center that reaches the bottom of the pint container. 13. Add the peanuts into the hole and press Mix-In button. 14. When the program is completed, turn the Outer Bowl and release it from the machine. 15. Transfer the ice cream into serving bowls and serve immediately.

Serving Suggestions: Serve with the garnishing of chopped peanuts.
Variation Tip: You can use strawberry jelly instead of grape jelly.
Nutritional Information per Serving: Calories: 349 | Fat: 23.1g | Sat Fat: 7.5g | Carbohydrates: 27.5g | Fiber: 2g | Sugar: 21.5g | Protein: 11.5g

Graham Cracker Ice Cream

Preparation Time: 30 minutes|Servings: 2

Ingredients:

½ cup whole milk

⅞ cup crushed graham crackers, divided

⅛ teaspoon kosher salt

2 egg yolks

1 tablespoon agave nectar

½ cup cream

Preparation:

1. Combine the whole milk, ⅝ cup crushed graham crackers, and salt in a mixing bowl. 2. Combine egg yolks and agave nectar in a medium saucepan. Whisk everything together. 3. Strain the graham cracker crumbs from the milk using a fine-mesh strainer set over the saucepan. 4. Press the graham crackers into the filter with a spoon to release any milk that has been absorbed. Toss in the cream and stir to mix. 5. Place the pot on the burner over medium heat and whisk continually. Cook until the temperature hits 165°F–175°F. 6. Transfer the mixture into a Ninja Creami pint. 7. Cover the container with a pint lid and freeze for 24 hours. 8. After 24 hours, remove the lid from the container and arrange it into the outer bowl of Ninja Creami. 9. Install the "Creamerizer Paddle" onto the lid of the outer bowl. 10. Then rotate the lid clockwise to lock. 11. Turn on the unit. 12. Then select the "ICE CREAM" function. 13. When the program is completed, with a spoon, create a 1½-inch wide hole in the center that reaches the bottom of the pint. 14. Add the remaining crushed graham crackers to the hole and select the "MIX-IN" function. 15. When the program is completed, turn the outer bowl and release it from the machine. 16. Serve in bowls.

Serving Suggestions: Top with caramel syrup.
Variation Tip: You can use coconut milk.
Nutritional Information per Serving: Calories: 349 | Fat: 21g| Sat Fat: 10g| Carbohydrates: 32g| Fiber: 1g| Sugar: 15g| Protein: 7.8g

Chocolate Chip Ice Cream

Preparation Time: 5 minutes|Servings: 2

Ingredients:

½ tablespoon cream cheese, softened

1/6 cup granulated sugar

½ teaspoon vanilla extract

⅜ cup heavy cream

½ cup whole milk

½ tablespoon mini chocolate chips

Preparation:

1. Microwave cream cheese for 10 seconds in a large microwave-safe bowl. 2. Combine the sugar and vanilla extract in a mixing bowl with a whisk or rubber spatula until the mixture resembles frosting, about 60 seconds. 3. Slowly whisk in the heavy cream and milk until smooth, and the sugar has dissolved. 4. Transfer the mixture into a Ninja Creami pint. 5. Cover the container with a pint lid and freeze for 24 hours. 6. After 24 hours, remove the lid from the container and arrange it into the outer bowl of Ninja Creami. 7. Install the "Creamerizer Paddle" onto the lid of the outer bowl. 8. Then rotate the lid clockwise to lock. 9. Turn on the unit. 10. Then select the "ICE CREAM" function. 11. When the program is completed, with a spoon, create a 1½-inch wide hole in the center that reaches the bottom of the pint. 12. Add the chocolate chips to the hole and select the "MIX-IN" function. 13. When the program is completed, turn the outer bowl and release it from the machine. 14. Serve in bowls.

Serving Suggestions: Top with chocolate chips.
Variation Tip: You can also add any fruit extract.
Nutritional Information per Serving: Calories: 190 | Fat: 11.3g| Sat Fat: 6g| Carbohydrates: 20g| Fiber: 0g| Sugar: 20g| Protein: 2.6g

Chocolate Nut Ice Cream

Preparation Time: 10 minutes|Servings: 6

Ingredients:

1 cup whole milk

¾ cup heavy cream

⅓ cup granulated sugar

2 tablespoons mini chocolate chips

2 tablespoons cocoa powder

½ cup brownies, chopped

½ cup walnuts, chopped

Preparation:

1. Place the ingredients in a blender. Mix well until smooth. 2. Pour the mixture into the Ninja CREAMi Pint and close it with the lid. 3. Place the pint into the freezer and freeze for 24 hours. 4. Once done, open the lid and set the pint into the outer bowl of the Ninja CREAMi. Place the Creamerizer Paddle into the outer bowl. 5. Lock the lid by rotating it clockwise. 6. Turn on the unit and then press the ICE CREAM button. 7. Once done, take out the bowl from the Ninja CREAMi. 8. Serve and enjoy your delicious ice cream!

Serving Suggestions: Serve with chocolate sauce on top.
Variation Tip: You can also add cranberries.
Nutritional Information per Serving: Calories: 269 | Fat: 16.7g | Sat Fat: 5.8g | Carbohydrates: 28.6g | Fiber: 1.3g | Sugar: 13.5g | Protein: 5.4g

Vanilla Blueberry Ice Cream

Preparation Time: 10 minutes|Servings: 6

Ingredients:

6 pie crusts
1 cup whole milk
¾ cup heavy cream
⅓ cup granulated sugar
1 large egg, beaten
½ cup frozen blueberries, thawed

Preparation:

1. Place the ingredients in a blender. Mix well until smooth. 2. Pour the mixture into the Ninja CREAMi Pint and close it with the lid. 3. Place the pint into the freezer for 24 hours. 4. Once frozen, remove the lid and set the pint into the outer bowl of the Ninja CREAMi. Set the Creamerizer Paddle into the outer bowl. 5. Lock the lid by rotating it clockwise. 6. Turn the unit on and then press the ICE CREAM button. 7. Once done, take out the bowl from the Ninja CREAMi. 8. Serve and enjoy.

Serving Suggestions: Serve with blueberry sauce on top.
Variation Tip: You can add some rolled oats to the mixture.
Nutritional Information per Serving: Calories: 109.5 | Fat: 70g | Sat Fat: 20g | Carbohydrates: 103.3g | Fiber: 3.4g | Sugar: 17.5g | Protein: 14.3g

Chocolate and Spinach Ice Cream

Preparation Time: 10 minutes|Servings: 2

Ingredients:

½ cup frozen spinach, thawed and squeezed dry
1 cup whole milk
½ cup granulated sugar
1 teaspoon mint extract
3–5 drops green food coloring
⅓ cup heavy cream
¼ cup chocolate chunks, chopped
¼ cup brownie, cut into 1-inch pieces

Preparation:

1. In a high-speed blender, add the spinach, milk, sugar, mint extract, and food coloring and pulse until the mixture is smooth. 2. Transfer the mixture to the Ninja CREAMi Pint. 3. Snap the lid on the pint and freeze it for 24 hours. 4. Remove the lid and assemble the unit as per the user instructions 5. Select the ICE CREAM function. 6. When the program is complete, use a spoon to create a 1½-inch wide hole in the center of the ice cream that reaches the bottom of the pint. 7. Add the chocolate chunks and brownie pieces to the hole and select the MIX-IN program. 8. When the program is complete, remove the outer bowl. 9. Serve in bowls.

Serving Suggestions: Top with sprinkles.
Variation Tip: You can also use coconut milk.
Nutritional Information per Serving: Calories: 243 | Fat: 10g | Sat Fat: 2g | Carbohydrates: 36g |Fiber: 0.4g | Sugar: 33g | Protein: 3.4g

Cherry Pudding Ice Cream

Preparation Time: 20 minutes|Servings: 2

Ingredients:

1/6 cup vanilla instant pudding mix
½ cup whole milk
1 tablespoon cream
¼ cup dark cherries
1-1 ½ tablespoons chocolate chips

Preparation:

1. Add the first four ingredients in a mixing bowl and whisk together until well incorporated, and the mixture has thickened somewhat. 2. Transfer the mixture into a Ninja Creami pint. 3. Cover the container with a pint lid and freeze for 24 hours. 4. After 24 hours, remove the lid from the container and arrange it into the outer bowl of Ninja Creami. 5. Install the "Creamerizer Paddle" onto the lid of the outer bowl. 6. Then rotate the lid clockwise to lock. 7. Turn on the unit. 8. Then select the "ICE CREAM" function. 9. When the program is completed, with a spoon, create a 1½-inch wide hole in the center that reaches the bottom of the pint. 10. Add the crushed chocolate chips to the hole and select the "MIX-IN" function. 11. When the program is completed, turn the outer bowl and release it from the machine. 12. Serve in bowls.

Serving Suggestions: Top with cherries.
Variation Tip: You can use any milk.
Nutritional Information per Serving: Calories: 104 | Fat: 4g| Sat Fat: 2g| Carbohydrates: 10g| Fiber: 0.2g| Sugar: 9g| Protein: 3g

Lavender Cookies & Cream Ice Cream

Preparation Time: 20 Minutes|Cook Time: 24 Hours and 20 Minutes|Serves: 2

Ingredients:
½ cup heavy cream
½ tablespoon dried culinary lavender
¼ teaspoon kosher salt
½ cup whole milk
¼ cup sweetened condensed milk
2 drops purple food coloring
¼ cup crushed chocolate wafer cookies

Preparation:
1. Whisk together the heavy cream, lavender, and salt in a medium saucepan. 2. Steep the mixture for 10 minutes over low heat, stirring every 2 minutes to prevent bubbling. 3. Using a fine-mesh strainer, drain the lavender from the heavy cream into a large mixing basin. Discard the lavender. 4. Combine the milk, sweetened condensed milk, and purple food coloring in a large mixing bowl. Whisk until the mixture is completely smooth. 5. Pour the base into an empty CREAMi Pint. Place the Pint into an ice bath. Once cooled, place the storage lid on the Pint and freeze for 24 hours. 6. Remove the Pint from the freezer and remove its lid. Place Pint in outer bowl, install Creamerizer Paddle in outer bowl lid, and lock the lid assembly onto the outer bowl. Select ICE CREAM. 7. When the process is done, create a 1½-inch wide hole that reaches the bottom of the Pint with a spoon. It's okay if your treat exceeds the max fill line. Add crushed wafer cookies to the hole and process again using the MIX-IN program. 8. When processing is complete, remove ice cream from Pint and serve immediately, topped with extra crumbled wafers if desired.

Serving Suggestion: Serve immediately.
Variation Tip: You can use this mix-in with different flavor ice creams.
Nutritional Information per Serving: Calories 180 | Protein 3g | Carbohydrate 19g | Dietary Fiber 0.5g | Sugar 14g | Fat 16g | Sodium 60mg

Caramel Oreo Ice Cream

Preparation Time: 5 minutes|Servings: 4

Ingredients:
1 cup chocolate milk
6 tablespoons chocolate syrup
¾ cup caramel creamer
4 Oreos, crushed

Preparation:
1. Mix together the chocolate milk, chocolate until well combined. 2. Transfer the mixture into a Ninja Creami pint. 3. Cover the container with a pint lid and freeze for 24 hours. 4. After 24 hours, remove the lid from the container and arrange it into the outer bowl of Ninja Creami. 5. Install the "Creamerizer Paddle" onto the lid of the outer bowl. 6. Then rotate the lid clockwise to lock. 7. Turn on the unit. 8. Then select the "ICE CREAM" function. 9. When the program is completed, with a spoon, create a 1½-inch wide hole in the center that reaches the bottom of the pint. 10. Add the crushed Oreos to the hole and select the "MIX-IN" function. 11. When the program is completed, turn the outer bowl and release it from the machine. 12. Serve in bowls.

Serving Suggestions: Top with Oreos.
Variation Tip: You can use fruit sweetener.
Nutritional Information per Serving: Calories: 246 | Fat: 15g| Sat Fat: 1.5g| Carbohydrates: 24g| Fiber: 3.5g| Sugar: 17g| Protein: 7g

Pineapple Ginger Ice Cream

Preparation Time: 10 minutes|Servings: 2

Ingredients:
¾ cup crushed pineapple
1 tablespoon fresh ginger, grated
1 cup whole milk
¾ cup heavy cream
⅓ cup granulated sugar

Preparation:
1. Put all the ingredients in a blender. Mix well until smooth. 2. Pour the mixture into the Ninja CREAMi Pint and close the lid. 3. Place the pint into the freezer and freeze for 24 hours. 4. Once done, remove the lid, and place the pint into the outer bowl of the Ninja CREAMi. Set the Creamerizer Paddle into the outer bowl. 5. Lock the lid by rotating it clockwise. 6. Turn the unit on and press the ICE CREAM button. 7. Once done, take out the bowl from the Ninja CREAMi. 8. Serve and enjoy.

Serving Suggestions: Serve with some maple syrup on top.
Variation Tip: Add some cinnamon for a tasty variation.
Nutritional Information per Serving: Calories: 394 | Fat: 20.9g | Sat Fat: 12.7g | Carbohydrates: 50.1g | Fiber: 1.2g | Sugar: 46g | Protein: 5.4g

Pea and Jam Ice Cream

Preparation Time: 5 minutes|Servings: 4

Ingredients:

¾ cup whole milk
½ cup frozen peas, thawed
¼ cup granulated sugar
3 tablespoons grape jam
2 tablespoons peanut butter powder
1 teaspoon vanilla extract

Purple gel food coloring to desired color (about 5–7 drops)
½ cup heavy cream
¼ cup roasted peanuts, chopped, for mix-in
¼ cup frozen mixed berries, for mix-in

Preparation:

1. Combine the milk, peas, sugar, grape jam, peanut butter powder, and vanilla extract in a blender pitcher. Blend on high for about 60 seconds or until the mixture is perfectly smooth. If using, blend in the food coloring until it's thoroughly blended. 2. Transfer the mixture to the Ninja CREAMi Pint. 3. Snap the lid on the pint and freeze it for 24 hours. 4. Remove the lid and assemble the unit as per the user instructions. 5. Select the ICE CREAM program. 6. When the program is complete, use a spoon to create a 1½-inch wide hole in the center of the ice cream that reaches the bottom of the pint. 7. Add the chopped roasted peanuts and mixed berries to the hole and select the MIX-IN program. 8. When the program is complete, remove the outer bowl. 9. Serve in bowls.

Serving Suggestions: Top with grapes.
Variation Tip: You can use any milk.
Nutritional Information per Serving: Calories: 202 | Fat: 11g | Sat Fat: 5g | Carbohydrates: 22g |Fiber: 3g | Sugar: 15g | Protein: 8g

Vanilla Ice Cream With Chocolate Chips

Preparation Time: 5 Minutes|Cook Time: 24 Hours and 5 Minutes|Serves: 4

Ingredients:

1 tablespoon cream cheese, softened
⅓ cup granulated sugar
1 teaspoon vanilla extract

¾ cup heavy cream
1 cup whole milk
¼ cup mini chocolate chips, for mix-in

Preparation:

1. Microwave the cream cheese for 10 seconds in a large microwave-safe bowl. With a rubber spatula, blend in the sugar and vanilla extract until the mixture resembles frosting, about 60 seconds. 2. Slowly whisk in the heavy cream and milk until smooth and the sugar has dissolved. 3. Pour the base into an empty CREAMi Pint. Place the storage lid on the Pint and freeze for 24 hours. 4. Remove the Pint from the freezer and remove the lid from the Pint. Place the Pint in the outer bowl, install the Creamerizer Paddle onto the outer bowl lid, and lock the lid assembly on the outer bowl. Select ICE CREAM. 5. With a spoon, create a 1½-inch wide hole that reaches the bottom of the Pint. During this process, it's okay for your treat to press above the max fill line. Add chocolate chips to the hole in the Pint and process again using the MIX-IN program. 6. When processing is complete, remove the ice cream from the Pint.

Serving Suggestion: Serve immediately.
Variation Tip: Add more chocolate and nuts if you prefer.
Nutritional Information per Serving: Calories 160 | Protein 2g | Carbohydrate 18g | Dietary Fiber 1g | Sugar 17g | Fat 8g | Sodium 46mg

Cookies & Cream Ice Cream

Preparation Time: 5 Minutes|Cook Time: 24 Hours and 5 Minutes|Serves: 2

Ingredients:

½ tablespoon cream cheese, softened
¼ cup granulated sugar
½ teaspoon vanilla extract

½ cup heavy cream
½ cup whole milk
1½ chocolate sandwich cookies, broken, for mix-in

Preparation:

1. Microwave the cream cheese for 10 seconds in a large microwave-safe bowl. Combine the sugar and vanilla extract in a mixing bowl and whisk or scrape together until the mixture resembles frosting, about 60 seconds. 2. Slowly whisk in the heavy cream and milk until smooth and the sugar has dissolved. 3. Pour the base into an empty CREAMi Pint. Place storage lid on the Pint and freeze for 24 hours. 4. Remove the Pint from the freezer and remove the lid from the Pint. Place the Pint in the outer bowl, install Creamerizer Paddle onto the outer bowl lid, and lock the lid assembly on the outer bowl. Select ICE CREAM. 5. With a spoon, create a 1½-inch wide hole that reaches the bottom of the Pint. During this process, it's okay for your treat to go above the max fill line. Add the broken chocolate sandwich cookies to the hole and process again using the MIX-IN program. 6. When processing is complete, remove the ice cream from the Pint and serve immediately.

Serving Suggestion: Serve immediately.
Variation Tip: Add in any ice cream of your choice.
Nutritional Information per Serving: Calories 140 | Protein 2g | Carbohydrate 23g | Dietary Fiber 0.5g | Sugar 15g | Fat 4g | Sodium 86mg

Strawberry Oreo Ice Cream

Preparation Time: 5 minutes|Servings: 4

Ingredients:

1 tablespoon cream cheese, softened
⅓ cup granulated sugar
1 teaspoon vanilla extract
6 strawberries, chopped
¾ cup heavy cream, whipped
1 cup whole milk
6 Oreos, broken

Preparation:

1. Microwave the cream cheese for 10 seconds in a large microwave-safe bowl. 2. Combine the sugar and vanilla extract in a mixing bowl and whisk or scrape together until the mixture resembles frosting, about 60 seconds. 3. Slowly whisk in the heavy cream, chopped strawberries, and milk until smooth, and the sugar has dissolved. 4. Transfer the mixture into a Ninja Creami pint. 5. Cover the container with a pint lid and freeze for 24 hours. 6. After 24 hours, remove the lid from the container and arrange it into the outer bowl of Ninja Creami. 7. Install the "Creamerizer Paddle" onto the lid of the outer bowl. 8. Then rotate the lid clockwise to lock. 9. Turn on the unit. 10. Then select the "ICE CREAM" function. 11. When the program is completed, with a spoon, create a 1½-inch wide hole in the center that reaches the bottom of the pint. 12. Add the broken Oreos to the hole and select the "MIX-IN" function. 13. When the program is completed, turn the outer bowl and release it from the machine. 14. Serve in bowls.

Serving Suggestions: Top with crushed cookies.
Variation Tip: You can use any flavored cookies.
Nutritional Information per Serving: Calories: 188 | Fat: 11g| Sat Fat: 6g| Carbohydrates: 20g| Fiber: 0g| Sugar: 20g| Protein: 2g

Snack Mix Ice Cream

Preparation Time: 15 minutes|Cooking Time: 10 seconds|Servings: 4

Ingredients:

1 tablespoon cream cheese, softened
⅓ cup granulated sugar
½ teaspoon vanilla extract
1 cup whole milk
¾ cup heavy cream
2 tablespoons sugar cone pieces
1 tablespoon mini pretzels
1 tablespoon potato chips, crushed

Preparation:

1. In a large microwave-safe bowl, add the cream cheese and microwave on High for about ten seconds. 2. Remove from the microwave and stir until smooth. 3. Add the sugar and vanilla extract and with a wire whisk, beat until the mixture looks like frosting. 4. Slowly add the milk and heavy cream and beat until well combined. 5. Transfer the mixture into an empty Ninja CREAMi pint container. 6. Cover the container with storage lid and freeze for 24 hours. 7. After 24 hours, remove the lid from container and arrange into the Outer Bowl of Ninja CREAMi. 8. Install the Creamerizer Paddle onto the lid of Outer Bowl. 9. Then rotate the lid clockwise to lock. 10. Press Power button to turn on the unit. 11. Then press Ice Cream button. 12. When the program is completed, with a spoon, create a 1½-inch wide hole in the center that reaches the bottom of the pint container. 13. Add the cone pieces, pretzels and potato chips into the hole and press Mix-In button. 14. When the program is completed, turn the Outer Bowl and release it from the machine. 15. Transfer the ice cream into serving bowls and serve immediately.

Serving Suggestions: Serve with the drizzling of chocolate syrup.
Variation Tip: Use full-fat cream cheese.
Nutritional Information per Serving: Calories: 182 | Fat: 4.3g|Sat Fat: 2g|Carbohydrates: 32.8g|Fiber: 0.3g|Sugar: 23.3g|Protein: 3.6g

Nuts & Jelly Ice Cream

Preparation Time: 25 minutes|Servings: 2

Ingredients:

2 large egg yolks
1 ½ tablespoons granulated sugar
1/6 cup heavy cream
½ cup whole milk
1 ½ tablespoons grape jelly
⅛ cup honey roasted nuts, chopped, for mix-in

Preparation:

1. Add the egg yolks and sugar in a small saucepan. Whisk until everything is well blended and the sugar has dissolved. 2. Stir together the heavy cream, milk and grape jelly in a saucepan. 3. Using a rubber spatula, constantly swirl the contents of the saucepan over medium heat. 4. Cook until the temperature hits 165°F -175°F. 5. Remove the base from the heat and let it cool. 6. Transfer the mixture into a Ninja Creami pint. 7. Cover the container with a pint lid and freeze for 24 hours. 8. After 24 hours, remove the lid from the container and arrange it into the outer bowl of Ninja Creami. 9. Install the "Creamerizer Paddle" onto the lid of the outer bowl. 10. Then rotate the lid clockwise to lock. 11. Turn on the unit. 12. Then select the "ICE CREAM" function. 13. When the program is completed, with a spoon, create a 1½-inch wide hole in the center that reaches the bottom of the pint. 14. Add the ¼ cup honey-roasted nuts bites to the hole and select the "MIX-IN" function. 15. When the program is completed, turn the outer bowl and release it from the machine. 16. Serve in bowls.

Serving Suggestions: Top with roasted peanuts.
Variation Tip: You can use fruit sweetener.
Nutritional Information per Serving: Calories: 347 | Fat: 22g| Sat Fat: 7g| Carbohydrates: 27g| Fiber: 1.9g| Sugar: 21g| Protein: 11g

Lavender Cookie Ice Cream

Preparation Time: 15 minutes|Cooking Time: 10 minutes|Servings: 4

Ingredients:

¾ cup heavy cream

1 tablespoon dried culinary lavender

⅛ teaspoon salt

¾ cup whole milk

½ cup sweetened condensed milk

4 drops purple food coloring

⅓ cup chocolate wafer cookies, crushed

Preparation:

1. In a medium saucepan, add heavy cream, lavender and salt and mix well. 2. Place the saucepan over low heat and steep, covered for about ten minutes, stirring after every two minutes. 3. Remove from the heat and through a fine-mesh strainer, strain the cream mixture into a large bowl. 4. Discard the lavender leaves. 5. In the bowl of cream mixture, add the milk, condensed milk and purple food coloring and beat until smooth. 6. Transfer the mixture into an empty Ninja CREAMi pint container. 7. Cover the container with storage lid and freeze for 24 hours. 8. After 24 hours, remove the lid from container and arrange into the Outer Bowl of Ninja CREAMi. 9. Install the Creamerizer Paddle onto the lid of Outer Bowl. 10. Then rotate the lid clockwise to lock. 11. Press Power button to turn on the unit. 12. Then press Ice Cream button. 13. When the program is completed, with a spoon, create a 1½-inch wide hole in the center that reaches the bottom of the pint container. 14. Add the crushed cookies the hole and press Mix-In button. 15. When the program is completed, turn the Outer Bowl and release it from the machine. 16. Transfer the ice cream into serving bowls and serve immediately.

Serving Suggestions: Serve with the garnishing of chocolate chunks.
Variation Tip: Use organic food color.
Nutritional Information per Serving: Calories: 229 | Fat: 13.2g|Sat Fat: 8.1g|Carbohydrates: 23.5g|Fiber: 0g|Sugar: 23.2g|Protein: 5g

Rum Raisin Ice Cream

Preparation Time: 23 Minutes|Cook Time: 24 Hours and 23 Minutes|Serves: 4

Ingredients:

3 large egg yolks

¼ cup dark brown sugar (or coconut sugar)

1 tablespoon light corn syrup

½ cup heavy cream

1 cup whole milk

1 teaspoon rum extract

⅓ cup raisins

¼ cup dark or spiced rum

Preparation:

1. In a small saucepan, combine the egg yolks, sugar, and corn syrup. Whisk until everything is well mixed and the sugar has dissolved. Whisk together the heavy cream and milk until smooth. 2. Stir the mixture frequently with a whisk or a rubber spatula in a saucepan over medium-low heat. Using an instant-read thermometer, cook until the temperature hits 165°F–175°F. 3. Remove the base from heat, stir in the rum extract, then pour through a fine-mesh strainer into an empty CREAMi Pint. Place into an ice bath. Once cooled, place the storage lid on the Pint and freeze for 24 hours. 4. While the base is cooling, prepare the mix-in. Add the raisins and rum to a small bowl and microwave for 1 minute. Let cool, then drain the remaining rum. Cover and set aside. 5. Remove the Pint from the freezer and remove its lid. Place the Pint in the outer bowl, install the Creamerizer Paddle onto the outer bowl lid, and lock the lid assembly on the outer bowl. Select ICE CREAM. 6. With a spoon, create a 1½-inch wide hole that reaches the bottom of the Pint. Add the mixed raisins to the hole and process again using the MIX-IN program. 7. When processing is complete, remove the ice cream from the Pint.

Serving Suggestion: Serve immediately.
Variation Tip: Add nuts if you like.
Nutritional Information per Serving: Calories 160 | Protein 2g | Carbohydrate 18g | Dietary Fiber 1g | Sugar 18g | Fat 7g | Sodium 45mg

Creamy Cookie Ice Cream

Preparation Time: 40 minutes | Servings: 2

Ingredients:

⅝ cup whole milk
1 cup frosted cookies, crushed, divided
½ tablespoon cream cheese, softened
1/6 cup granulated sugar
1 teaspoon vanilla extract
⅜ cup heavy cream

Preparation:

1. Combine the milk and 1 cup of crushed cookies in a medium mixing bowl. Allow 30 minutes for the cookie flavor to absorb the milk, stirring regularly. 2. Microwave the cream cheese for 10 seconds in a large microwave-safe bowl. 3. Combine the granulated sugar and vanilla extract in a mixing bowl with a whisk or rubber spatula until smooth. Set aside. 4. After 30 minutes, sift the milk and cookie mixture over the cream cheese mixture in a fine-mesh strainer. 5. Gently press down on the cookies to release the milk, and then toss the drenched cookies away. 6. Whisk the heavy cream into the bowl until it is completely mixed. 7. Transfer the mixture into a Ninja Creami pint. 8. Cover the container with a pint lid and freeze for 24 hours. 9. After 24 hours, remove the lid from the container and arrange it into the outer bowl of Ninja Creami. 10. Install the "Creamerizer Paddle" onto the lid of the outer bowl. 11. Then rotate the lid clockwise to lock. 12. Turn on the unit. 13. Then select the "ICE CREAM" function. 14. When the program is completed, with a spoon, create a 1½-inch wide hole in the center that reaches the bottom of the pint. 15. Add the remaining crushed cookies to the hole and select the "MIX-IN" function. 16. When the program is completed, turn the outer bowl and release it from the machine. 17. Serve in bowls.

Serving Suggestions: Top with crushed cookies.
Variation Tip: You can skip the cheese.
Nutritional Information per Serving: Calories: 199 | Fat: 11g| Sat Fat: 7g| Carbohydrates: 21g| Fiber: 0g| Sugar: 20g| Protein: 3g

Pretzel Ice Cream

Preparation Time: 10 minutes | Servings: 2

Ingredients:

½ tablespoon cream cheese, softened
1/6 cup sugar
⅜ cup cream
½ cup whole milk
1 tablespoon vanilla extract
½ tablespoon mini pretzels

Preparation:

1. Microwave the cream cheese for 10 seconds in a large microwave-safe bowl. 2. Combine the sugar and vanilla extract in a mixing bowl and whisk together until the mixture resembles frosting, about 60 seconds. 3. Slowly whisk in the cream and milk until smooth, and the sugar has dissolved. 4. Transfer the mixture into a Ninja Creami pint. 5. Cover the container with a pint lid and freeze for 24 hours. 6. After 24 hours, remove the lid from the container and arrange it into the outer bowl of Ninja Creami. 7. Install the "Creamerizer Paddle" onto the lid of the outer bowl. 8. Then rotate the lid clockwise to lock. 9. Turn on the unit. 10. Then select the "ICE CREAM" function. 11. When the program is completed, with a spoon, create a 1½-inch wide hole in the center that reaches the bottom of the pint. 12. Add the mini pretzels to the hole and select the "MIX-IN" function. 13. When the program is completed, turn the outer bowl and release it from the machine. 14. Serve in bowls.

Serving Suggestions: Top with more pretzels.
Variation Tip: You can use coconut milk.
Nutritional Information per Serving: Calories: 416 | Fat: 14g| Sat Fat: 7.7g| Carbohydrates: 62g| Fiber: 1g| Sugar: 23g| Protein: 8g

Mojito Sorbet

Preparation Time: 2 Minutes|Cook Time: 24 Hours and 5 Minutes|Serves: 8

Ingredients:

½ cup water
½ cup white sugar
¼ cup mint leaves, packed
1 teaspoon grated lime zest
½ cup freshly squeezed lime juice
¾ cup citrus-flavored sparkling water
1 tablespoon rum (optional)

Preparation:

1. Add all ingredients to a bowl and mix until the sugar is dissolved. Pour into the ninja CREAMi Pint container and freeze on a level surface in a cold freezer for a full 24 hours. 2. After 24 hours, remove the Pint from the freezer. Remove the lid. 3. Place the Ninja CREAMi Pint into the outer bowl. Place the outer bowl with the Pint in it into the ninja CREAMi machine and turn until the outer bowl locks into place. Push the SORBET button. During the SORBET function, the sorbet will mix together and become very creamy. This should take approximately 2 minutes. 4. Once the SORBET function has ended, turn the outer bowl and release it from the ninja CREAMi machine. 5. Your sorbet is ready to eat! Enjoy!

Serving Suggestion: Serve immediately.
Variation Tip: Add fresh mint on top.
Nutritional Information per Serving: Calories 56 | Protein 0.1g | Carbohydrate 14g | Dietary Fiber 0.2g | Sugar 12g | Fat 0.1g | Sodium 1.6mg

Blueberry Lemon Sorbet

Preparation Time: 5 Minutes|Cook Time: 24 Hours and 5 Minutes|Serves: 1

Ingredients:

1 tablespoon cream cheese (room temperature or microwaved for 10–20 seconds)
¼ cup milk
1½ cups lemonade
⅓ cup blueberries (fresh or frozen)

Preparation:

1. In a medium mixing bowl, whisk together the softened cream cheese and the milk. Make an effort to integrate the two as much as possible. Some little bits of cream cheese may remain, but that's fine as long as they're small. 2. Add the lemonade and stir thoroughly. 3. Pour the mixture into a ninja CREAMi Pint container, add the blueberries and freeze on a level surface in a cold freezer for a full 24 hours. 4. After 24 hours, remove the Pint from the freezer. Remove the lid. 5. Place the Ninja CREAMi Pint into the outer bowl. Place the outer bowl with the Pint in it into the ninja CREAMi machine and turn until the outer bowl locks into place. Push the SORBET button. During the SORBET function, the sorbet will mix together and become very creamy. This should take approximately 2 minutes. 6. Once the SORBET function has ended, turn the outer bowl and release it from the ninja CREAMi machine. 7. Your sorbet is ready to eat! Enjoy! 8. Place the outer bowl with the Pint back into the ninja CREAMi machine and lock it into place if the sorbet isn't quite creamy enough. Select the RE-SPIN option. Remove the outer bowl from the Ninja CREAMi after the RE-SPIN cycle is complete.

Serving Suggestion: Serve immediately.
Variation Tip: Add nuts of your choice.
Nutritional Information per Serving: Calories 246 | Protein 3g | Carbohydrate 56g | Dietary Fiber 1g | Sugar 50g | Fat 7g | Sodium 96mg

Sweeet and Sour Mango Sorbet

Preparation Time: 15 minutes|Servings: 4

Ingredients:

4 cups mangoes, peeled, pitted and chopped
½ cup water
⅓-½ cup sugar
¼ cup fresh lime juice
2 tablespoons Chamoy

Preparation:

1. In a high-speed blender, add mangoes and water and pulse until smooth. 2. Through a fine-mesh strainer, strain the mango puree into a large bowl. 3. Add the sugar, lime juice and chamoy and stir to combine. 4. Transfer the mixture into an empty Ninja CREAMi pint container. 5. Cover the container with storage lid and freeze for 24 hours. 6. After 24 hours, remove the lid from container and arrange into the Outer Bowl of Ninja CREAMi. 7. Install the Creamerizer Paddle onto the lid of Outer Bowl. 8. Then rotate the lid clockwise to lock. 9. Press Power button to turn on the unit. 10. Then press Sorbet button. 11. When the program is completed, turn the Outer Bowl and release it from the machine. 12. Transfer the sorbet into serving bowls and serve immediately.

Serving Suggestions: Serve with the topping of coconut.
Variation Tip: make sure to use ripe mango.
Nutritional Information per Serving: Calories: 168 | Fat: 5.6g|Sat Fat: 0.2g|Carbohydrates: 42g| Fiber: 2.6g|Sugar: 39.2g|Protein: 1.4g

Lemony Herb Sorbet

Preparation Time: 15 minutes|Cooking Time: 6 minutes|Servings: 4

Ingredients:

½ cup water
¼ cup granulated sugar
2 large fresh dill sprigs, stemmed
2 large fresh basil sprigs, stemmed
1 cup ice water
2 tablespoons fresh lemon juice

Preparation:
1. In a small saucepan, add sugar and water and over medium heat and cook for about five minutes or until the sugar is dissolved, stirring continuously. 2. Stir in the herb sprigs and remove from the heat. 3. Add the ice water and lemon juice and stir to combine. 4. Transfer the mixture into an empty Ninja CREAMi pint container. 5. Cover the container with storage lid and freeze for 24 hours. 6. After 24 hours, remove the lid from container and arrange into the Outer Bowl of Ninja CREAMi. 7. Install the Creamerizer Paddle onto the lid of Outer Bowl. 8. Then rotate the lid clockwise to lock. 9. Press Power button to turn on the unit. 10. Then press Sorbet button. 11. When the program is completed, turn the Outer Bowl and release it from the machine. 12. Transfer the sorbet into serving bowls and serve immediately.

Serving Suggestions: Serve with the garnishing of fresh herbs.
Variation Tip: Use herbs of your choice.
Nutritional Information per Serving: Calories: 51 | Fat: 0.1g|Sat Fat: 0g.1|Carbohydrates: 13.1g|Fiber: 0.1g|Sugar: 12.7g|Protein: 0.2g

Pineapple Basil Sorbet

Preparation Time: 10 minutes|Servings: 6

Ingredients:

16 ounces canned pineapple chunks, with juice
1 teaspoon lemon juice
1 teaspoon lemon zest
1 small piece of ginger, sliced
1 teaspoon basil leaves
⅓ cup white caster sugar

Preparation:
1. Place all the ingredients in a blender. Mix well until smooth. 2. Pour the mixture into the Ninja CREAMi Pint and close the lid. 3. Place the pint into the freezer and freeze for 24 hours. 4. Once done, open the lid, place the pint into the outer bowl of the Ninja CREAMi, and set the Creamerizer Paddle into the outer bowl. 5. Lock the lid by rotating it clockwise. 6. Turn the unit on and press the SORBET button. 7. Once done, take out the bowl from the Ninja CREAMi. 8. Serve and enjoy this yummy sorbet.

Serving Suggestions: Serve with mint leaves on top.
Variation Tip: You can add white rum for variation.
Nutritional Information per Serving: Calories: 34 | Fat: 0.1g | Sat Fat: 0g | Carbohydrates: 8.9g | Fiber: 0.5g | Sugar: 5.9g | Protein: 0.1g

Lime Sorbet

Preparation Time: 10 minutes|Servings: 4

Ingredients:

¾ cup beer
⅔ cup water
½ cup fresh lime juice
¼ cup granulated sugar

Preparation:
1. In a high-speed blender, add all the ingredients and pulse until smooth. 2. Set aside for about five minutes. 3. Transfer the mixture into an empty Ninja CREAMi pint container. 4. Cover the container with storage lid and freeze for 24 hours. 5. After 24 hours, remove the lid from container and arrange into the Outer Bowl of Ninja CREAMi. 6. Install the Creamerizer Paddle onto the lid of Outer Bowl. 7. Then rotate the lid clockwise to lock. 8. Press Power button to turn on the unit. 9. Then press Sorbet button. 10. When the program is completed, turn the Outer Bowl and release it from the machine. 11. Transfer the sorbet into serving bowls and serve immediately.

Serving Suggestions: Serve with the garnishing of lime zest.
Variation Tip: For best result, use canned Mexican beer.
Nutritional Information per Serving: Calories: 69 | Fat: 0g|Sat Fat: 0g|Carbohydrates: 14.4g|Fiber: 0g|Sugar: 12.5g|Protein: 0.2g

Passionfruit Peach Sorbet

Preparation Time: 10 minutes|Servings: 4

Ingredients:

1 cup passionfruit seltzer
3 tablespoons agave nectar
1 (15¼-ounce) can peaches in heavy syrup, drained

Preparation:
1. In a bowl, add the seltzer and agave and beat until agave is dissolved. 2. Place the peaches into an empty Ninja CREAMi pint container and top with seltzer mixture. 3. Cover the container with storage lid and freeze for 24 hours. 4. After 24 hours, remove the lid from container and arrange into the Outer Bowl of Ninja CREAMi. 5. Install the Creamerizer Paddle onto the lid of Outer Bowl. 6. Then rotate the lid clockwise to lock. 7. Press Power button to turn on the unit. 8. Then press Sorbet button. 9. When the program is completed, turn the Outer Bowl and release it from the machine. 10. Transfer the sorbet into serving bowls and serve immediately.

Serving Suggestions: Serve with the garnishing of fresh mint leaves.
Variation Tip: Agave nectar can be replaced with maple syrup.
Nutritional Information per Serving: Calories: 271 | Fat: 1.5g|Sat Fat: 0g|Carbohydrates: 65.4g|Fiber: 9.5g|Sugar: 64.6g|Protein: 5.3g

Pomegranate & Blueberry Sorbet

Preparation Time: 10 minutes|Servings: 4

Ingredients:
1 (15-ounce) can blueberries in light syrup   ½ cup pomegranate juice

Preparation:
1. In an empty Ninja CREAMi pint container, place the blueberries and top with syrup 2. Add in the pomegranate juice and stir to combine. 3. Cover the container with storage lid and freeze for 24 hours. 4. After 24 hours, remove the lid from container and arrange into the Outer bowl of Ninja CREAMi. 5. Install the Creamerizer Paddle onto the lid of Outer Bowl. 6. Then rotate the lid clockwise to lock. 7. Press Power button to turn on the unit. 8. Then press Sorbet button. 9. When the program is completed, turn the Outer Bowl and release it from the machine. 10. Transfer the sorbet into serving bowls and serve immediately.

Serving Suggestions: Serve with garnishing of fresh blueberries.
Variation Tip: Use sweetened pomegranate juice.
Nutritional Information per Serving: Calories: 101 | Fat: 0.4g|Sat Fat: 0g|Carbohydrates: 25.2g| Fiber: 2.6g|Sugar: 19g|Protein: 0.8g

Mixed Berries Sorbet

Preparation Time: 10 minutes|Servings: 4

Ingredients:
1 cup blueberries   1 cup strawberries, hulled and
1 cup raspberries   quartered

Preparation:
1. In an empty Ninja CREAMi pint container, place the berries and with a potato masher, mash until well combined. 2. Cover the container with storage lid and freeze for 24 hours. 3. After 24 hours, remove the lid from container and arrange into the outer bowl of Ninja CREAMi. 4. Install the Creamerizer Paddle onto the lid of Outer Bowl. 5. Then rotate the lid clockwise to lock. 6. Press Power button to turn on the unit. 7. Then press Sorbet button. 8. When the program is completed, turn the Outer Bowl and release it from the machine. 9. Transfer the sorbet into serving bowls and serve immediately.

Serving Suggestions: Serve with the garnishing of chocolate chips.
Variation Tip: You can use berries of your choice.
Nutritional Information per Serving: Calories: 48 | Fat: .40g|Sat Fat: 0g|Carbohydrates: 11.7g| Fiber: 3.6g|Sugar: 6.7g|Protein: 0.9g

Banana Sorbet

Preparation Time: 10 minutes|Cooking Time: minutes|Servings: 2

Ingredients:
2 large bananas   Water, as required

Preparation:
1. Place the ingredients in a blender. Mix well until smooth. 2. Pour the mixture into the Ninja CREAMi Pint and close it with the lid. 3. Place the pint into the freezer and freeze for 24 hours. 4. Once done, open the lid and place the pint into the outer bowl of the Ninja CREAMi. Set the Creamerizer Paddle into the outer bowl. 5. Lock the lid by rotating it clockwise. 6. Turn on the unit and press the SORBET button. 7. Once done, take out the bowl from the Ninja CREAMi. 8. Serve and enjoy this yummy sorbet.

Serving Suggestions: Serve with banana slices on top.
Variation Tip: Sprinkle with some ground cinnamon.
Nutritional Information per Serving: Calories: 61 | Fat: 0.2g | Sat Fat: 0.1g | Carbohydrates: 15.5g | Fiber: 1.8g | Sugar: 8.3g | Protein: 0.7g

Cherry Cola Sorbet

Preparation Time: 10 minutes|Servings: 4

Ingredients:
1½ cups cola   ¼ cup water
⅓ cup maraschino cherries   1 tablespoon lime juice
⅓ cup spiced rum

Preparation:
1. Place the cherries, rum, water, and lime juice into a blender pitcher and blend on high until smooth, about 60 seconds. 2. Pour the mixture into the Ninja CREAMi Pint and snap on the lid. 3. Place the pint into the freezer and freeze for 24 hours. 4. Remove the lid and assemble the unit as per the user instructions. 5. Select the SORBET program. 6. Once the program is complete, remove the outer bowl. 7. Serve and enjoy.

Serving Suggestions: Top with cherries.
Variation Tip: You can add some honey.
Nutritional Information per Serving: Calories: 95 | Fat: 0.1g | Sat Fat: 0g | Carbohydrates: 13g |Fiber: 0.3g | Sugar: 12g | Protein: 0.2g

Watermelon Lime Sorbet

Preparation Time: 10 minutes|Servings: 4

Ingredients:

3½ cups seedless watermelon chunks

2 teaspoons lime juice
¼ cup warm water

Preparation:
1. Place all the ingredients in a blender. Mix well until smooth. 2. Pour the mixture into the Ninja CREAMi Pint and close the lid. 3. Place the pint into the freezer and freeze for 24 hours. 4. Once done, open the lid and place the pint into the outer bowl of the Ninja CREAMi. Set the Creamerizer Paddle into the outer bowl. 5. Lock the lid by rotating it clockwise. 6. Turn on the unit and press the SORBET button. 7. Once done, take out the bowl from the Ninja CREAMi. 8. Serve and enjoy your yummy sorbet.

Serving Suggestions: Add some watermelon slices and serve.
Variation Tip: You can add honey for more flavor.
Nutritional Information per Serving: Calories: 177 | Fat: 0.8g | Sat Fat: 0.4g | Carbohydrates: 44.3g | Fiber: 2.3g | Sugar: 36.2g | Protein: 3.5g

Coconut Mango Sorbet

Preparation Time: 10 minutes|Servings: 6

Ingredients:

3 ripe mangoes, sliced
2 tablespoons lemon juice
1 tablespoon lemon zest

3 cups dairy-free coconut milk ice cream
A few mint leaves

Preparation:
1. Add all the ingredients to a blender. Mix well until smooth. 2. Pour the mixture into the Ninja CREAMi Pint and close the lid. 3. Place the pint into the freezer and freeze for 24 hours. 4. Once done, open the lid and place the pint into the outer bowl of the Ninja CREAMi. Set the Creamerizer Paddle into the outer bowl. 5. Lock the lid by rotating it clockwise. 6. Turn the unit on and press the SORBET button. 7. Once done, take out the bowl from the Ninja CREAMi. 8. Serve and enjoy this yummy sorbet.

Serving Suggestions: Serve with sliced lemon and mint leaves.
Variation Tip: Add vanilla essence for a taste variation.
Nutritional Information per Serving: Calories: 184 | Fat: 4.2g | Sat Fat: 3.2g | Carbohydrates: 39.6g | Fiber: 6.3g | Sugar: 32g | Protein: 1.9g

Peach Bellini Sorbet

Preparation Time: 5 minutes|Servings: 4

Ingredients:

2 cups peach juice or nectar
1 cup champagne or white

sparkling wine
¼ cup granulated sugar

Preparation:
1. Whisk together the peach juice/nectar and champagne/wine in a medium saucepan over medium heat. Bring to a boil, then reduce the heat to low and cook for 10 minutes or until the liquid is reduced to 2 cups. 2. Whisk in the sugar until it's completely dissolved. 3. Remove from the heat and let the mixture cool. 4. Pour the mixture into the Ninja CREAMi Pint and snap on the lid. 5. Place the pint into the freezer and freeze for 24 hours. 6. Remove the lid and assemble the unit as per the user instructions. 7. Select the SORBET program. 8. When the program is complete, remove the outer bowl. 9. Serve and enjoy!

Serving Suggestions: Top with peach slices.
Variation Tip: You can add honey for sweetness.
Nutritional Information per Serving: Calories: 47 | Fat: 0g | Sat Fat: 0g | Carbohydrates: 12g |Fiber: 0g | Sugar: 12g | Protein: 0g

Elderflower Sorbet

Preparation Time: 10 minutes|Servings: 6

Ingredients:

1 cup white caster sugar
3¾ cups gooseberry, topped and tailed
5 tablespoons undiluted elderflower cordial
1 egg white

Preparation:

1. Add all the ingredients into a blender. Mix well until smooth. 2. Pour the mixture into the Ninja CREAMi Pint and close the lid. 3. Place the pint into the freezer and freeze for 24 hours. 4. Once done, open the lid and place the pint into the outer bowl of the Ninja CREAMi. Set the Creamerizer Paddle into the outer bowl. 5. Lock the lid by rotating it clockwise. 6. Turn the unit on and press the SORBET button. 7. Once done, take out the bowl from the Ninja CREAMi. 8. Serve and enjoy this yummy sorbet.

Serving Suggestions: Serve with some mint leaves on top.
Variation Tip: Add coconut extract for a taste variation.
Nutritional Information per Serving: Calories: 127 | Fat: 0.4g | Sat Fat: 0.3g | Carbohydrates: 44g | Fiber: 1.2g | Sugar: 23.2g | Protein: 3.5g

Peach Sorbet

Preparation Time: 5 Minutes|Cook Time: 24 Hours and 5 Minutes|Serves: 1

Ingredients:

12 ounces canned peaches (in chunks)

Preparation:

1. Pour the canned peaches (with their liquid) into a ninja CREAMi Pint container and freeze on a level surface in a cold freezer for a full 24 hours. 2. After 24 hours, remove the Pint from the freezer. Remove the lid. 3. Place the Ninja CREAMi Pint into the outer bowl. Place the outer bowl with the Pint in it into the ninja CREAMi machine and turn until the outer bowl locks into place. Push the SORBET button. During the SORBET function, the sorbet will mix together and become very creamy. This should take approximately 2 minutes. 4. Once the SORBET function has ended, turn the outer bowl and release it from the ninja CREAMi machine. 5. Your sorbet is ready to eat! Enjoy!

Serving Suggestion: Serve immediately.
Variation Tip: Add some fresh mint.
Nutritional Information per Serving: Calories 169 | Protein 4g | Carbohydrate 41g | Dietary Fiber 6g | Sugar 27g | Fat 1g | Sodium 256mg

Pumpkin Sorbet

Preparation Time: 5 minutes|Servings: 2

Ingredients:

½ can pumpkin
1 tablespoon lime juice

Preparation:

1. Pour fruit into a Ninja Creami pint and close the container with a lid. 2. Place the pint into a freezer and freeze for 24 hours. 3. Once done, open the pint and set it into an outer bowl of Ninja Creami and set the 'Creamerizer Paddle' into the outer bowl. 4. Lock the lid by rotating it clockwise. 5. Turn on the unit and then select the 'SORBET' function. 6. Once it is done, take out the bowl from Ninja Creami. 7. Serve and enjoy your sorbet.

Serving Suggestions: Top with fruit slices.
Variation Tip: You can add honey.
Nutritional Information per Serving: Calories: 52 | Fat: 0g| Sat Fat: 0g| Carbohydrates: 13g| Fiber: 1g| Sugar: 12g| Protein: 0.9g

Coconut Lime Sorbet

Preparation Time: 30 Minutes|Cook Time: 24 Hours and 30 Minutes|Serves: 5

Ingredients:

1 (7 ounces) can coconut cream
½ cup coconut water
¼ cup lime juice
½ tablespoon lime zest
¼ teaspoon coconut extract (optional)

Preparation:

1. Combine the coconut cream, coconut water, lime juice, lime zest, and coconut extract in a mixing bowl. Cover with plastic wrap and refrigerate for at least 1 hour, or until the flavors have melded. 2. Add the mixture to the Ninja CREAMi Pint container and freeze on a level surface in a cold freezer for a full 24 hours. 3. After 24 hours, remove the Pint from the freezer. Remove the lid. 4. Place the Ninja CREAMi Pint into the outer bowl. Place the outer bowl with the Pint in it into the ninja CREAMi machine and turn until the outer bowl locks into place. Push the SORBET button. During the SORBET function, the sorbet will mix together and become very creamy. This should take approximately 2 minutes. 5. Once the SORBET function has ended, turn the outer bowl and release it from the ninja CREAMi machine. 6. Your sorbet is ready to eat! Enjoy!

Serving Suggestion: Serve immediately.
Variation Tip: Add some chocolate shavings on top.
Nutritional Information per Serving: Calories 194 | Protein 1g | Carbohydrate 30g | Dietary Fiber 0.5g | Sugar 27g | Fat 9g | Sodium 36mg

Lychee Sorbet

Preparation Time: 10 minutes|Servings: 4

Ingredients:

2 cans lychees in syrup
2 teaspoons caster sugar
Thumb-size piece ginger, sliced
1 egg white

Preparation:
1. Place all the ingredients in a blender. Mix well until smooth. 2. Pour the mixture into the Ninja CREAMi Pint and close it with the lid. 3. Place the pint into the freezer and freeze for 24 hours. 4. Once done, open the lid and place the pint into the outer bowl of the Ninja CREAMi. Set the Creamerizer Paddle into the outer bowl. 5. Lock the lid by rotating it clockwise. 6. Turn the unit on and press the SORBET button. 7. Once done, take out the bowl from the Ninja CREAMi. 8. Serve and enjoy this yummy sorbet.

Serving Suggestions: Serve with candied ginger slices on top.
Variation Tip: You can add maple syrup if you like.
Nutritional Information per Serving: Calories: 18 | Fat: 0g | Sat Fat: 0g | Carbohydrates: 3.6g | Fiber: 0g | Sugar: 2.1g | Protein: 0.9g

Lemon Zesty Sorbet

Preparation Time: 10 minutes|Servings: 2

Ingredients:

¾ cup white caster sugar
A thick strip of lemon peel

3 cups lemons juice

Preparation:
1. Place the ingredients in a blender. Mix well until smooth. 2. Pour the mixture into the Ninja CREAMi Pint and close it with the lid. 3. Place the pint into the freezer and freeze for 24 hours. 4. Once done, open the lid and place the pint into the outer bowl of the Ninja CREAMi. Set the Creamerizer Paddle into the outer bowl. 5. Lock the lid by rotating it clockwise. 6. Turn the unit on and press the SORBET button. 7. Once done, take out the bowl from the Ninja CREAMi. 8. Serve and enjoy this yummy sorbet.

Serving Suggestions: Serve with lemon zest on top.
Variation Tip: You can also add white rum if you like.
Nutritional Information per Serving: Calories: 24 | Fat: 0.6g | Sat Fat: 0.6g | Carbohydrates: 3.5g | Fiber: 0.6g | Sugar: 3.1g | Protein: 0.6g

Strawberries & Champagne Sorbet

Preparation Time: 15 Minutes|Cook Time: 24 Hours and 15 Minutes|Serves: 3

Ingredients:

1 (2 ounces) packet strawberry-flavored gelatin (such as Jell-O)
¾ cup boiling water
½ cup light corn syrup
3 fluid ounces champagne
1 egg whites, slightly beaten

Preparation:
1. Dissolve the gelatin in boiling water in a bowl. Beat in the corn syrup, champagne, and egg whites. 2. Put the mixture into the ninja CREAMi Pint container and freeze on a level surface in a cold freezer for a full 24 hours. 3. After 24 hours, remove the Pint from the freezer. Remove the lid. 4. Place the Ninja CREAMi Pint into the outer bowl. Place the outer bowl with the Pint in it into the ninja CREAMi machine and turn until the outer bowl locks into place. Push the SORBET button. During the SORBET function, the sorbet will mix together and become very creamy. This should take approximately 2 minutes. 5. Once the SORBET function has ended, turn the outer bowl and release it from the ninja CREAMi machine. 6. Your sorbet is ready to eat! Enjoy!

Serving Suggestion: Serve immediately.
Variation Tip: Add some fresh mint.
Nutritional Information per Serving: Calories 196 | Protein 2.5g | Carbohydrate 46g | Dietary Fiber 0.5g | Sugar 23g | Fat 5g | Sodium 106mg

Orange Star Anise Sorbet

Preparation Time: 10 minutes|Servings: 2

Ingredients:

2 cups orange juice
2 teaspoons star anise

½ cup caster sugar

Preparation:

1. Add the ingredients to a blender. Mix well until smooth. 2. Pour the mixture into the Ninja CREAMi Pint and close the lid. 3. Place the pint into the freezer and freeze for 24 hours. 4. Once done, open the lid and place the pint into the outer bowl of the Ninja CREAMi. Set the Creamerizer Paddle into the outer bowl. 5. Lock the lid by rotating it clockwise. 6. Turn the unit on and press the SORBET button. 7. Once done, take out the bowl from the Ninja CREAMi. 8. Serve and enjoy this yummy sorbet.

Serving Suggestions: Serve with mint leaves on top.
Variation Tip: You can also add some strawberry syrup for a taste variation.
Nutritional Information per Serving: Calories: 153 | Fat: 0.4g | Sat Fat: 0.1g | Carbohydrates: 38.4g | Fiber: 0.4g | Sugar: 35.4g | Protein: 1g

Plum Sorbet

Preparation Time: 10 minutes|Servings: 4

Ingredients:
1 (20-ounce) can plums

Preparation:

1. Place the plums into an empty Ninja CREAMi pint container. 2. Cover the container with storage lid and freeze for 24 hours. 3. After 24 hours, remove the lid from container and arrange into the Outer Bowl of Ninja CREAMi. 4. Install the Creamerizer Paddle onto the lid of Outer Bowl. 5. Then rotate the lid clockwise to lock. 6. Press Power button to turn on the unit. 7. Then press Sorbet button. 8. When the program is completed, turn the Outer Bowl and release it from the machine. 9. Transfer the sorbet into serving bowls and serve immediately.

Serving Suggestions: Serve with the garnishing of coconut flakes.
Variation Tip: You can use peaches sin this recipe too.
Nutritional Information per Serving: Calories: 150 | Fat: 1g|Sat Fat: 0g|Carbohydrates: 40g|Fiber: 4.5g|Sugar: 35g|Protein: 2.5g

Chocolate Sorbet

Preparation Time: 5 Minutes|Cook Time: 24 Hours and 5 Minutes|Serves: 2

Ingredients:

½ cup white sugar
⅓ cup unsweetened cocoa powder
1 pinch sea salt
1 cups water

1 tablespoon brewed espresso or strong coffee
½ teaspoon almond extract
1 tablespoon coffee liqueur

Preparation:

1. Mix the sugar, cocoa powder, and sea salt in a large saucepan. Stir in water, espresso, and almond extract. Once the sugar has dissolved and the mixture is smooth, stir in the coffee liqueur. 2. Pour into a ninja CREAMi Pint container and freeze on a level surface in a cold freezer for a full 24 hours. 3. After 24 hours, remove the Pint from the freezer. Remove the lid. 4. Place the Ninja CREAMi Pint into the outer bowl. Place the outer bowl with the Pint in it into the ninja CREAMi machine and turn until the outer bowl locks into place. Push the SORBET button. During the SORBET function, the sorbet will mix together and become very creamy. This should take approximately 2 minutes. 5. Once the SORBET function has ended, turn the outer bowl and release it from the ninja CREAMi machine.

Serving Suggestion: Serve immediately.
Variation Tip: Add some chopped nuts if you prefer.
Nutritional Information per Serving: Calories 256 | Protein 3g | Carbohydrate 61g | Dietary Fiber 5g | Sugar 52g | Fat 2g | Sodium 63mg

Raspberry Strawberry Sorbet

Preparation Time: 10 minutes | Servings: 2

Ingredients:
2 strawberries, sliced
1 cup raspberries

2 cups water

Preparation:
1. Place the ingredients in a blender. Mix well until smooth. 2. Pour the mixture into the Ninja CREAMi Pint and close the lid. 3. Place the pint into the freezer and freeze for 24 hours. 4. Once done, open the lid and place the pint into the outer bowl of the Ninja CREAMi. Set the Creamerizer Paddle into the outer bowl. 5. Lock the lid by rotating it clockwise. 6. Turn the unit on and press the SORBET button. 7. Once done, take out the bowl from the Ninja CREAMi. 8. Serve and enjoy your yummy sorbet.

Serving Suggestions: Serve with chopped nuts on top.
Variation Tip: You can add honey for a taste variation.
Nutritional Information per Serving: Calories: 36 | Fat: 0.4g | Sat Fat: 0g | Carbohydrates: 8.3g | Fiber: 4.2g | Sugar: 3.3g | Protein: 0.8g

Boozy Passion Peach Sorbet

Preparation Time: 5 minutes | Servings: 4

Ingredients:
1 cup passion fruit seltzer
3 tablespoons raw agave nectar
1 can (15¼-ounce) peaches in

heavy syrup, drained and syrup discarded

Preparation:
1. Whisk the seltzer and agave together in a large bowl until the agave is dissolved. 2. Pour the peaches into the Ninja CREAMi Pint up to the MAX FILL line. Pour the seltzer and agave mixture over the peaches. 3. Snap the lid on the pint and freeze it for 24 hours. 4. Remove the lid and assemble the unit as per the user instructions. 5. Select the SORBET program. 6. When the program is complete, remove the outer bowl. 7. Serve and enjoy.

Serving Suggestions: Top with fresh mint.
Variation Tip: You can add in some real passion fruit pieces.
Nutritional Information per Serving: Calories: 18 | Fat: 0.2g | Sat Fat: 0g | Carbohydrates: 3g | Fiber: 0.6g | Sugar: 3g | Protein: 0.4g

Awesome Banana Sorbet

Preparation Time: 5 Minutes | Cook Time: 24 Hours and 5 Minutes | Serves: 2

Ingredients:
1 frozen banana
1 teaspoon cold water

2 teaspoons caramel sauce

Preparation:
1. Add the banana, water, and caramel sauce into the ninja CREAMi Pint container and freeze on a level surface in a cold freezer for a full 24 hours. 2. After 24 hours, remove the Pint from the freezer. Remove the lid. 3. Place the Ninja CREAMi Pint into the outer bowl. Place the outer bowl with the Pint in it into the ninja CREAMi machine and turn until the outer bowl locks into place. Push the SORBET button. During the SORBET function, the sorbet will mix together and become very creamy. This should take approximately 2 minutes. 4. Once the SORBET function has ended, turn the outer bowl and release it from the ninja CREAMi machine.

Serving Suggestion: Serve immediately.
Variation Tip: You can top the sorbet with flaked almonds.
Nutritional Information per Serving: Calories 70 | Protein 0.7g | Carbohydrate 18g | Dietary Fiber 1.6g | Sugar 7.2g | Fat 0.2g | Sodium 25mg

Italian Ice Sorbet

Preparation Time: 3 Minutes |Cook Time: 24 Hours and 5 Minutes|Serves: 1

Ingredients:
12 ounces lemonade
Sugar or your preferred sweetener to taste (optional)
If the lemonade you're using
is quite tart, use 6 ounces of lemonade and 6 ounces of water instead of 12 ounces of lemonade

Preparation:
1. Pour the lemonade (or lemonade and water mixture) into a ninja CREAMi Pint container and freeze on a level surface in a cold freezer for a full 24 hours. 2. After 24 hours, remove the Pint from the freezer. Remove the lid. 3. Place the Ninja CREAMi Pint into the outer bowl. Place the outer bowl with the Pint in it into the ninja CREAMi machine and turn until the outer bowl locks into place. Push the SORBET button. During the SORBET function, the sorbet will mix together and become very creamy. This should take approximately 2 minutes. 4. Once the SORBET function has ended, turn the outer bowl and release it from the ninja CREAMi machine.

Serving Suggestion: Serve immediately.
Variation Tip: Add some lemon zest.
Nutritional Information per Serving: Calories 236 | Protein 8g | Carbohydrate 58g | Dietary Fiber 0.5g | Sugar 54g | Fat 14g | Sodium 29mg

Blueberry Kiwi Sorbet

Preparation Time: 5 minutes|Servings: 4

Ingredients:
2 cups sliced blueberries
3-4 kiwis, peeled, small pieces
⅛ cup raw agave
¼ cup water

Preparation:
1. Combine the sliced blueberries, kiwi pieces, agave, and water in a blender and blend until fully smooth. 2. Pour mixture into a Ninja Creami pint and close the container with a lid. 3. Place the pint into a freezer and freeze for 24 hours. 4. Once done, open the pint and set it into an outer bowl of Ninja Creami and set the 'Creamerizer Paddle' into the outer bowl. 5. Lock the lid by rotating it clockwise. 6. Turn on the unit and then select the 'SORBET' function. 7. Once it is done,

take out the bowl from Ninja Creami. 8. Serve and enjoy your sorbet.

Serving Suggestions: Top with berries.
Variation Tip: You can add honey.
Nutritional Information per Serving: Calories: 90 | Fat: 0.3g| Sat Fat: 0g| Carbohydrates: 22g| Fiber: 3.2g| Sugar: 17g| Protein: 0.7g

Pear Sorbet

Preparation Time: 5 minutes|Servings: 4

Ingredients:
4 ounces pear

Preparation:
1. Pour pear juice into a Ninja Creami pint and close the container with a lid. 2. Place the pint into a freezer and freeze for 24 hours. 3. Once done, open the pint and set it into an outer bowl of Ninja Creami and set the 'Creamerizer Paddle' into the outer bowl. 4. Lock the lid by rotating it clockwise. 5. Turn on the unit and then select the 'SORBET' function. 6. Once it is done, take out the bowl from Ninja Creami. 7. Serve and enjoy sorbet.

Serving Suggestions: Top with fruit slices.
Variation Tip: You can add honey for more taste.
Nutritional Information per Serving: Calories: 9 | Fat: 0g| Sat Fat: 0g| Carbohydrates: 2.3g| Fiber: 0.3g| Sugar: 2g| Protein: 0.2g

Lima Beans Sorbet

Preparation Time: 5 minutes|Servings: 2

Ingredients:
¼ cup frozen lima beans, thawed
¼ cup granulated sugar
¼ cup lime juice
½ cup whole milk

Preparation:
1. In a blender, combine the lima beans, sugar, lime juice, and milk and blend on high for 60 seconds, or until totally smooth. 2. Pour mixture into a Ninja Creami pint and close the container with a lid. 3. Place the pint into a freezer and freeze for 24 hours. 4. Once done, open the pint and set it into an outer bowl of Ninja Creami and set the 'Creamerizer Paddle' into the outer bowl. 5. Lock the lid by rotating it clockwise. 6. Turn on the unit and then select the 'SORBET' function. 7. Once it is done, take out the bowl from Ninja Creami. 8. Serve and enjoy your sorbet.

Serving Suggestions: Top with fruit slices.
Variation Tip: You can use coconut milk.
Nutritional Information per Serving: Calories: 218 | Fat: 10.9g| Sat Fat: 8.6g| Carbohydrates: 30.7g| Fiber: 1g| Sugar: 26g| Protein: 2.2g

Pineapple Sorbet

Preparation Time: 5 Minutes|Cook Time: 24 Hours 5 Minutes|Serves: 1

Ingredients:
12 ounces canned pineapple

Preparation:
1. Pour the pineapple, with the liquid from the can, into a ninja CREAMi Pint container and freeze on a level surface in a cold freezer for a full 24 hours. 2. After 24 hours, remove the Pint from the freezer. Remove the lid. 3. Place the Ninja CREAMi Pint into the outer bowl. Place the outer bowl with the Pint in it into the ninja CREAMi machine and turn until the outer bowl locks into place. Push the SORBET button. During the SORBET function, the sorbet will mix together and become very creamy. This should take approximately 2 minutes. 4. Once the SORBET function has ended, turn the outer bowl and release it from the ninja CREAMi machine. 5. Your sorbet is ready to eat! Enjoy!

Serving Suggestion: Serve immediately.
Variation Tip: Add some fresh mint.
Nutritional Information per Serving: Calories 276 | Protein 2g | Carbohydrate 71g | Dietary Fiber 6g | Sugar 20g | Fat 1g | Sodium 56mg

Guava Sorbet

Preparation Time: 5 minutes|Servings: 2

Ingredients:
1 ½ cups chopped Guava   1/6 cup granulated sugar

Juice of ½ lime   1 tablespoon water

Preparation:
1. Add the chopped Guava, sugar, lime juice, and water in a blender and blend on high for 1 minute, or until smooth. For a smooth consistency, you can add more water. 2. Pour mixture into a Ninja Creami pint and close the container with a lid. 3. Place the pint into a freezer and freeze for 24 hours. 4. Once done, open the pint and set it into an outer bowl of Ninja Creami and set the 'Creamerizer Paddle' into the outer bowl. 5. Lock the lid by rotating it clockwise. 6. Turn on the unit and then select the 'SORBET' function. 7. Once it is done, take out the bowl from Ninja Creami. 8. Serve and enjoy your sorbet.

Serving Suggestions: Top with fruit slices.
Variation Tip: You can add honey.
Nutritional Information per Serving: Calories: 63 | Fat: 0g| Sat Fat: 0g| Carbohydrates: 16.7g| Fiber: 0g| Sugar: 16g| Protein: 0g

Lemon Thyme Sorbet

Preparation Time: 10 minutes|Servings: 2

Ingredients:
1 tablespoon invert sugar or corn syrup   6 sprigs thyme
1 cup water   ¾ cup lemon juice
½ cup white sugar   Zest of 2 lemons
     Pinch of salt

Preparation:
1. Combine the syrup, water, sugar, and thyme in a medium saucepan over medium heat. 2. Bring to a simmer and remove the thyme sprigs. 3. Add the lemon juice, lemon zest, and salt and stir to combine. 4. Remove the mixture from the heat and let it cool. 5. Pour the mixture into the Ninja CREAMi Pint and snap on the lid. 6. Place the pint into the freezer and freeze for 24 hours. 7. Remove the lid and assemble the unit as per the user instructions. 8. Select the SORBET program. 9. When the program is complete, remove the outer bowl. 10. Serve and enjoy.

Serving Suggestions: Top with lemon zest.
Variation Tip: You can add honey for more flavor.
Nutritional Information per Serving: Calories: 108 | Fat: 0g | Sat Fat: 0g | Carbohydrates: 24g |Fiber: 0.1g | Sugar: 33g | Protein: 0.2g

Mango Sorbet

Ingredients:

½ pound grapes

½ cup coconut water

1 tablespoon agave syrup

⅓ cup cold water

Preparation:

1. In a blender, combine grapes, coconut water, agave syrup, and water and blend on high for 60 seconds, or until totally smooth. 2. Pour mixture into a Ninja Creami pint and close the container with a lid. 3. Place the pint into a freezer and freeze for 24 hours. 4. Once done, open the pint and set it into an outer bowl of Ninja Creami and set the 'Creamerizer Paddle' into the outer bowl. 5. Lock the lid by rotating it clockwise. 6. Turn on the unit and then select the 'SORBET' function. 7. Once it is done, take out the bowl from Ninja Creami. 8. Serve and enjoy your sorbet.

Serving Suggestions: Top with fruit slices.

Variation Tip: You can add honey.

Nutritional Information per Serving: Calories: 60 | Fat: 0.1g| Sat Fat: 0.1g| Carbohydrates: 15g| Fiber: 0.8g| Sugar: 13g| Protein: 0.6g

Mix Fruit Sorbet

Preparation Time: 5 Minutes | Cook Time: 24 Hours and 5 Minutes | Serves: 6

Ingredients:

2 cups mango, peeled, seeded, and cubed

½ cup simple syrup

1 tablespoon fresh lime juice

Preparation:

1. Put the fruit, syrup, and fresh lime juice into the ninja CREAMi Pint container and freeze on a level surface in a cold freezer for a full 24 hours. 2. After 24 hours, remove the Pint from the freezer. Remove the lid. 3. Place the Ninja CREAMi Pint into the outer bowl. Place the outer bowl with the Pint in it into the ninja CREAMi machine and turn until the outer bowl locks into place. Push the SORBET button. During the SORBET function, the sorbet will mix together and become very creamy. This should take approximately 2 minutes. 4. Once the SORBET function has ended, turn the outer bowl and release it from the ninja CREAMi machine. 5. Your sorbet is ready to eat! Enjoy!

Serving Suggestion: Serve immediately.

Variation Tip: Add some fresh mint.

Nutritional Information per Serving: Calories 96 | Protein 0.4g | Carbohydrate 25g | Dietary Fiber 1.3g | Sugar 10g | Fat 0.2g | Sodium 2mg

Coconut Grape Sorbet

Preparation Time: 5 minutes|Servings: 1

Ingredients:

1 ripe banana, peeled, cut into ½-inch slices

¾ cup ripe pineapple, cut into

½-inch pieces

1 ¼ mangoes, peeled, cut into ½-inch pieces

Preparation:

1. Add fruits into a Ninja Creami pint. 2. Place the pint into a freezer and freeze for 24 hours. 3. Once done, open the pint and set it into an outer bowl of Ninja Creami and set the 'Creamerizer Paddle' into the outer bowl. 4. Lock the lid by rotating it clockwise. 5. Turn on the unit and then select the 'SORBET' function. 6. Once it is done, take out the bowl from Ninja Creami. 7. Serve and enjoy your sorbet.

Serving Suggestions: Top with fruit slices.

Variation Tip: You can add honey for more taste.

Nutritional Information per Serving: Calories: 203 | Fat: 0.6g| Sat Fat: 0.2g| Carbohydrates: 52g| Fiber: 7.6g| Sugar: 34g| Protein: 3g

Vanilla Banana Sorbet

Preparation Time: 5 minutes|Servings: 2

Ingredients:

¾ cup banana, slices

⅜ cup vanilla coffee creamer

½ teaspoon vanilla extract

Preparation:
1. In a blender, combine the banana slices, vanilla coffee creamer, and vanilla extract and blend on high for 60 seconds, or until totally smooth. 2. Pour mixture into a Ninja Creami pint and close the container with a lid. 3. Place the pint into a freezer and freeze for 24 hours. 4. Once done, open the pint and set it into an outer bowl of Ninja Creami and set the 'Creamerizer Paddle' into the outer bowl. 5. Lock the lid by rotating it clockwise. 6. Turn on the unit and then select the 'SORBET' function. 7. Once it is done, take out the bowl from Ninja Creami. 8. Serve and enjoy your sorbet.

Serving Suggestions: Top with fruit slices.
Variation Tip: You can add honey for more taste.
Nutritional Information per Serving: Calories: 119 | Fat: 3g| Sat Fat: 0g| Carbohydrates: 24g| Fiber: 0.7g| Sugar: 22.6g| Protein: 0.3g

Pineapple Sorbet

Preparation Time: 5 minutes|Servings: 4

Ingredients:

15 ounces pineapples

Preparation:
1. Pour 15 ounces of canned mangos with the liquid from the can into a Ninja Creami pint and close the container with a lid. 2. Place the pint into a freezer and freeze for 24 hours. 3. Once done, open the pint and set it into an outer bowl of Ninja Creami and set the 'Creamerizer Paddle' into the outer bowl. 4. Lock the lid by rotating it clockwise. 5. Turn on the unit and then select the 'SORBET' function. 6. Once it is done, take out the bowl from Ninja Creami. 7. Serve and enjoy your sorbet.

Serving Suggestions: Top with mango slices.
Variation Tip: You can add honey for more taste.
Nutritional Information per Serving: Calories: 140 | Fat: 0.2g| Sat Fat: 0.1g| Carbohydrates: 35g| Fiber: 1.2g| Sugar: 34g| Protein: 0.6g

Avocado Lime Sorbet

Preparation Time: 10 minutes|Servings: 4

Ingredients:

¾ cup water

1 pinch sea salt

2 tablespoons light corn syrup

⅔ cup granulated sugar

3 ounces fresh lime juice

1 large ripe avocado, skin and core removed

Preparation:
1. Whisk together the water, sea salt, and corn syrup in a medium saucepan over medium heat. Gradually add the sugar, stirring constantly. Bring to a boil, then turn off the heat. 2. Allow the mixture to cool completely before using. Once the mixture has cooled, combine it with the lime juice and avocado in a blender pitcher and blend until smooth, about 60 seconds. 3. Pour the mixture into the Ninja CREAMi Pint and snap on the lid. 4. Place the pint into the freezer and freeze for 24 hours. 5. Remove the lid and assemble the unit as per the user instructions. 6. Select the SORBET program. 7. When the program is complete, remove the outer bowl. 8. Serve and enjoy sorbet.

Serving Suggestions: Top with lime wedges.
Variation Tip: You can add a few berries for extra flavor.
Nutritional Information per Serving: Calories: 260 | Fat: 9g | Sat Fat: 2g | Carbohydrates: 46g |Fiber: 3g | Sugar: 36g | Protein: 1g

Pina Colada Sorbet

Preparation Time: 10 minutes|Servings: 2

Ingredients:

¾ cup pina colada mix
¼ cup rum

2 tablespoons granulated sugar
1½ cups frozen pineapple chunks

Preparation:
1. Combine all the ingredients in a blender pitcher and blend on high for 60 seconds or until smooth. 2. Pour the mixture into the Ninja CREAMi Pint and snap on the lid. 3. Place the pint into the freezer and freeze for 24 hours. 4. Remove the lid and assemble the unit as per the user instructions. 5. Select the SORBET program. 6. When the program is complete, remove the outer bowl. 7. Serve and enjoy!

Serving Suggestions: Top with pineapple chunks.
Variation Tip: You can add honey for sweetness.
Nutritional Information per Serving: Calories: 134 | Fat: 0.1g | Sat Fat: 0g | Carbohydrates: 24g |Fiber: 1g | Sugar: 23g | Protein: 0.4g

Pomegranate & Cherry Sorbet

Preparation Time: 5 minutes|Servings: 2

Ingredients:

½ can cherries

¼ cup pomegranate juice

Preparation:
1. Pour cherries and juice into a Ninja Creami pint and close the container with a lid. 2. Place the pint into a freezer and freeze for 24 hours. 3. Once done, open the pint and set it into an outer bowl of Ninja Creami and set the 'Creamerizer Paddle' into the outer bowl. 4. Lock the lid by rotating it clockwise. 5. Turn on the unit and then select the 'SORBET' function. 6. Once it is done, take out the bowl from Ninja Creami. 7. Serve and enjoy sorbet.

Serving Suggestions: Top with fruit slices.
Variation Tip: You can add honey for more taste.
Nutritional Information per Serving: Calories: 110 | Fat: 0.5g| Sat Fat: 0g| Carbohydrates: 28g| Fiber: 2.8g| Sugar: 23g| Protein: 1.2g

Strawberry Lime Sorbet

Preparation Time: 5 minutes|Servings: 1

Ingredients:

4 tablespoons lime juice
2 ounces rum

½ cup frozen strawberries
½ cup simple syrup

Preparation:
1. Pour all ingredients into a Ninja Creami pint and close the container with a lid. 2. Place the pint into a freezer and freeze for 24 hours. 3. Once done, open the pint and set it into an outer bowl of Ninja Creami and set the 'Creamerizer Paddle' into the outer bowl. 4. Lock the lid by rotating it clockwise. 5. Turn on the unit and then select the 'SORBET' function. 6. Once it is done, take out the bowl from Ninja Creami. 7. Serve and enjoy your sorbet.

Serving Suggestions: Top with fruit slices.
Variation Tip: You can add honey.
Nutritional Information per Serving: Calories: 310 | Fat: 1.5g| Sat Fat: 0.9g| Carbohydrates: 63g| Fiber: 0.8g| Sugar: 52g| Protein: 0g

Apricot Sorbet

Preparation Time: 5 minutes | Servings: 1

Ingredients:
1 ½ cup apricot, cubed   2 tablespoons coconut water

Preparation:
1. Pour all ingredients into a Ninja Creami pint and close the container with a lid. 2. Place the pint into a freezer and freeze for 24 hours. 3. Once done, open the pint and set it into an outer bowl of Ninja Creami and set the 'Creamerizer Paddle' into the outer bowl. 4. Lock the lid by rotating it clockwise. 5. Turn on the unit and then select the 'SORBET' function. 6. Once it is done, take out the bowl from Ninja Creami. 7. Serve and enjoy your sorbet.

Serving Suggestions: Top with lime juice.
Variation Tip: You can use any syrup.
Nutritional Information per Serving: Calories: 318 | Fat: 0g| Sat Fat: 0g| Carbohydrates: 76.8g| Fiber: 0.3g| Sugar: 72.3g| Protein: 0.6g

Mango and Lime Sorbet

Preparation Time: 10 minutes | Servings: 1

Ingredients:
1 cup chopped mangoes   ⅛ cup sugar
⅛ cup water   Tajin, as desired
1/16 cup lime juice

Preparation:
1. Puree mangoes and water in a high-powered blender. Using a fine-mesh strainer, filter the liquid. 2. Pour the mango base into a large mixing bowl and whisk in the lime juice and sugar. 3. Pour mixture into a Ninja Creami pint and close the container with a lid. 4. Place the pint into a freezer and freeze for 24 hours. 5. Once done, open the pint and set it into an outer bowl of Ninja Creami and set the 'Creamerizer Paddle' into the outer bowl. 6. Lock the lid by rotating it clockwise. 7. Turn on the unit and then select the 'SORBET' function. 8. Once it is done, take out the bowl from Ninja Creami. 9. Serve and enjoy your sorbet.

Serving Suggestions: Sprinkle tajin on top.
Variation Tip: You can add Camoy.
Nutritional Information per Serving: Calories: 380 | Fat: 0.6g| Sat Fat: 0.2g| Carbohydrates: 99g| Fiber: 2.5g| Sugar: 97g| Protein: 1.7g

Strawberry Sorbet

Preparation Time: 10 minutes | Servings: 4

Ingredients:
6 ounces daiquiri mix   ½ cup frozen strawberries
2 ounces rum   ½ cup simple syrup

Preparation:
1. In an empty Ninja CREAMi pint container, add all the ingredients and mix well. 2. Cover the container with storage lid and freeze for 24 hours. 3. After 24 hours, remove the lid from container and arrange into the Outer Bowl of Ninja CREAMi. 4. Install the Creamerizer Paddle onto the lid of Outer Bowl. 5. Then rotate the lid clockwise to lock. 6. Press Power button to turn on the unit. 7. Then press Sorbet button. 8. When the program is completed, turn the Outer Bowl and release it from the machine. 9. Transfer the sorbet into serving bowls and serve immediately.

Serving Suggestions: Serve with the garnishing of fresh strawberry slices.
Variation Tip: Don't thaw the strawberries.
Nutritional Information per Serving: Calories: 330 | Fat: 0.1g|Sat Fat: 0g|Carbohydrates: 72.6g|Fiber: 0.4g|Sugar: 37.7g|Protein: 0.1g

Strawberry, Beet, and Citrus Sorbet

Preparation Time: 10 minutes|Servings: 4

Ingredients:
2 ⅔ cups strawberries, stemmed and quartered
⅓ cup cooked beets, quartered
⅓ cup granulated sugar
⅓ cup orange juice

Preparation:
1. Combine all the ingredients in a blender pitcher and blend on high for 60 seconds or until smooth. 2. Pour the mixture into the Ninja CREAMi Pint and snap on the lid. 3. Place the pint into the freezer and freeze for 24 hours. 4. Remove the lid and assemble the unit as per the user instructions. 5. Select the SORBET program. 6. When the program is complete, remove the outer bowl. 7. Serve and enjoy.

Serving Suggestions: Top with strawberry chunks.
Variation Tip: You can add honey for more sweetness.
Nutritional Information per Serving: Calories: 109 | Fat: 0.4g | Sat Fat: 0g | Carbohydrates: 26g |Fiber: 2.3g | Sugar: 21g | Protein: 1g

Mixed Berry Sorbet

Preparation Time: 10 minutes|Servings: 4

Ingredients:
1 cup blueberries
1 cup raspberries
1 cup strawberries, stemmed and quartered

Preparation:
1. Put the ingredients in the Ninja CREAMi Pint and snap on the lid. 2. Place the pint into the freezer and freeze for 24 hours. 3. Remove the lid and assemble the unit as per the user instructions. 4. Select the SORBET program. 5. When the program is complete, remove the outer bowl. 6. Serve and enjoy.

Serving Suggestions: Top with fresh berries.
Variation Tip: You can add lime juice for more taste.
Nutritional Information per Serving: Calories: 48 | Fat: 0.4g | Sat Fat: 0g | Carbohydrates: 11g |Fiber: 3.6g | Sugar: 6.7g | Protein: 0.9g

Conclusion

The NINJA CREAMI is a multi-functional appliance. You can make ice cream at home using this appliance. It has different modes such as ice cream, sorbet, lite ice cream, gelato, smoothie bowl, milkshake, mix-ins, re-spin, etc. You can make your favorite ice cream using this appliance. Now, you didn't need to purchase a separate appliance for sorbet, ice cream, and gelato. All features are present in the appliance. In this cookbook, you will get delicious recipes for ice creams, milkshakes, smoothie bowls, gelato, sorbets, etc. There are a lot of benefits of using NINJA CREAMI, such as it takes less time to prepare ice cream, the cleaning process is simple, and it has a make-ahead feature. I hope you love this book. Thank you for purchasing it.

Appendix Measurement Conversion Chart

VOLUME EQUIVALENTS (LIQUID)

US STANDARD	US STANDARD (OUNCES)	METRIC (APPROXIMATE)
2 tablespoons	1 fl.oz	30 mL
¼ cup	2 fl.oz	60 mL
½ cup	4 fl.oz	120 mL
1 cup	8 fl.oz	240 mL
1½ cup	12 fl.oz	355 mL
2 cups or 1 pint	16 fl.oz	475 mL
4 cups or 1 quart	32 fl.oz	1 L
1 gallon	128 fl.oz	4 L

VOLUME EQUIVALENTS (DRY)

US STANDARD	METRIC (APPROXIMATE)
⅛ teaspoon	0.5 mL
¼ teaspoon	1 mL
½ teaspoon	2 mL
¾ teaspoon	4 mL
1 teaspoon	5 mL
1 tablespoon	15 mL
¼ cup	59 mL
½ cup	118 mL
¾ cup	177 mL
1 cup	235 mL
2 cups	475 mL
3 cups	700 mL
4 cups	1 L

TEMPERATURES EQUIVALENTS

FAHRENHEIT(F)	CELSIUS (C) (APPROXIMATE)
225 °F	107 ℃
250 °F	120 ℃
275 °F	135 ℃
300 °F	150 ℃
325 °F	160 ℃
350 °F	180 ℃
375 °F	190 ℃
400 °F	205 ℃
425 °F	220 ℃
450 °F	235 ℃
475 °F	245 ℃
500 °F	260 ℃

WEIGHT EQUIVALENTS

US STANDARD	METRIC (APPROXINATE)
1 ounce	28 g
2 ounces	57 g
5 ounces	142 g
10 ounces	284 g
15 ounces	425 g
16 ounces (1 pound)	455 g
1.5pounds	680 g
2pounds	907 g